$\mathcal{W}$e make a living by what we get,
but we make a life
by what we give.

—*Winston Churchill*

The 1990
Quick Job-Hunting
(And Career-Changing) Map

How to Create
A Picture of

Your Ideal Job
or
Next Career

Richard N. Bolles

Ten Speed Press

Introduction

I<small>N</small> ORDER TO HUNT FOR YOUR IDEAL JOB, or even something close to your ideal job, you must have a picture of it, in your head. The clearer the picture, the easier it will be to hunt for it. The purpose of this booklet is to guide you as you draw that picture.

We have chosen a "Flower" as the model for that picture. While such expressions as "plugging in," "turning on," and other common phrases portray you (implicitly) as a machine, you are actually much more like a Flower than a machine. That is to say, you flourish in some job-environments, but wither in others. Therefore, the purpose of putting together this Flower Picture of yourself is to help you identify what kind of a work climate you will flourish in, and thus do your very best work. Your twin goals should be to be as happy as you can be at your job, while at the same time you do your most effective work.

The small picture of our Flower model on the next page gives you an overview. That picture of the Flower, however, isn't large enough, nor does each petal have enough detail, to be really useful as a worksheet.

The actual worksheets, dealing with one petal at a time, are scattered throughout the remainder of this booklet. You will deal with the petals in a *logical* order of learning, beginning with the ones that are easiest to fill out, and working on through to the harder ones.

The order in which you will work on the eight petals is:

1. Physical Setting
2. Spiritual or Emotional Setting
3. My Favorite Skills -- what I like to do with *Things*, *People* and/or *Information*
4. My Favorite Kinds of People I Like to Use These Skills with
5. My Favorite Kinds of Information I Like to Use These Skills with
6. My Favorite Kinds of Things I Like to Use These Skills with
7. Outcomes: Immediate and Long-range
8. Rewards: Salary, Level and Other

And when you are done, you will put all the petals together, so that they form one complete Flower picture of your Ideal Job. Okay? Then, get out your pen or pencil and *let's get started*.

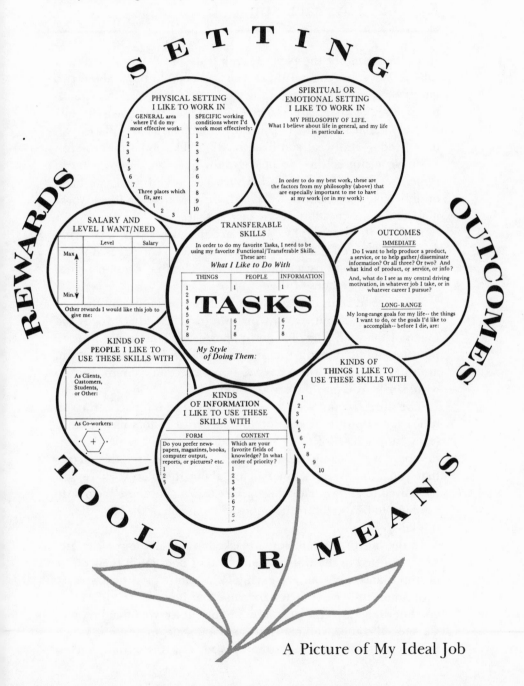

A Picture of My Ideal Job

Step One: Physical Setting

In order to fill out the petal dealing with The Physical Setting I
Like to Work In (pages 10–11), you will need to think about two
questions: your ideal Geography, and your ideal Working Conditions. Both of these are essentially exercises which search your
memory. That is to say, if you can remember all the places you
have lived -- and what you liked or didn't like about them -- you
will have answered the Ideal Geography question. And if you can
remember all the places you have worked -- and what you liked
or didn't like about them -- you will have answered the Ideal Working Conditions question. It's as easy as that.

First, to the Geography. Where are the places you have lived,
and what did you like or dislike about them? On pages 8-9 is a
chart to help you answer this question. The first column is (obviously) for the names of the towns or cities.

The second column is for you to list all the things you disliked
and still dislike about that city or town (e.g., "cloudy or foggy too
much of the year," "terrible newspaper," etc.). You do not need to
put these things directly opposite the name of the city or town you
are thinking of. Put them *anywhere* in the second column. But do
write small! You may have a lot to list.

The third column serves two purposes. The top part is for you
to list the **opposite** of each of your negative factors in column 2
(e.g., "sunny most of the year," "good newspaper," etc.). The bottom part of that same column is for you to list any positive factors
that you instantly remember liking about the places where you
have lived (e.g., "we had a big yard," etc.). Again, these factors do
not have to be listed directly opposite the name of the city you are
thinking of.

In the fourth column, you are asked to put all the positive factors you listed in the third column (top or bottom) in their order
of importance for you. For example, if "sunny most of the year"
is the most important factor for you, that becomes #1. If "has a
good newspaper" is the next most important for you, that becomes
#2, etc. Of course, you may find some difficulty in deciding which
Positive factor is most important to you, which is second, and so

on; if that is the case, we urge you to use the Prioritizing Grids which you will find on pages 13 and 14, complete with instructions.

The fifth column requires your friends to help you. You read to them the list of Positive factors that you have arranged, in order, in the fourth column, and see what cities or towns they can think of, that have these characteristics. Don't stumble over two factors that seem to be contradictory, like "sunny all year round" and "skiing nearby." There's usually an answer (like, "Palm Springs with the tram up Mt. San Jacinto to the snow"). When your friends are through suggesting places, pick the one you like best, next best, and third best, and put them on the bottom left side of the petal on page 10f. If you don't know enough about them, put your three favorites in any order, and write away to their chambers of commerce, to find out more about them. The library also can help!

The last three columns are only to be used if you have a wife, husband, or partner, and you are doing joint decision-making about where you eventually want to move to. In that case, your partner will need to photocopy the Geography chart (before you fill it out, obviously) and do their own first five columns. If your preferred geographical areas turn out to be identical, then you are done with the chart. But if they don't, then go on to column #6 and copy your partner's positive factors from his or her column #4.

Now, on to column #7. Merge together, there, your "Ranking of My Positives" and your partner's ranking. Your factors, obviously, are numbered 1, 2, 3, 4, 5, etc. while your partner's are numbered, a, b, c, d, e, etc. You will notice that column #7 asks you first to list your partner's top priority, then your top one, then your partner's second priority, then your second one, etc.

When done, move on to column #8. It involves exactly the same procedure as column #5. Show column #7 to all your friends and ask them what cities or towns they think of, when they read this (combined) list of factors. Again, don't be put off by apparently contradictory factors. There's usually some place, somewhere, that can give you both factors.

Incidentally, you may have looked at this chart and sort of shrugged your shoulders, because you already know your geographical destination, and by name. It's either where you already are, or some place you both *have to* move to, or some place you both would love to move to. Nonetheless, try filling out columns #1 through #4, anyway. It helps a lot if you know, in that city or town, which characteristics you like best (or you each like best) -- and in what order.

My/Our Geographical

Decision Making for Just You

Column 1 Names of Places I Have Lived	Column 2 From the Past: Negatives	Column 3 Translating the Nega- tives into Positives	Column 4 Ranking of My Positives
	Factors I Disliked and Still Dislike about That Place		1.
			2.
			3.
			4.
			5.
			6.
			7.
			8.
			9.
			10.
		Factors I Liked and Still Like about That Place	11.
			12.
			13.
			14.
			15.

Preferences

	Decision Making for You and a Partner		
Column 5 Places Which Fit These Criteria	*Column 6* Ranking of His/Her Preferences	*Column 7* Combining Our Two Lists (Columns 4 & 6)	*Column 8* Places Which Fit These Criteria
	a.	a. 1.	
	b.	b. 2.	
	c.	c. 3.	
	d.	d. 4.	
	e.	e. 5.	
	f.	f. 6.	
	g.	g. 7.	
	h.	h. 8.	
	i.	i. 9.	
	j.	j. 10.	
	k.	k. 11.	
	l.	l. 12.	
	m.	m. 13.	
	n.	n. 14.	
	o.	o. 15.	

The First Petal

The Physical Setting
I Like to Work In

GENERAL
Geographical Factors

The geographical area which would please me most, and therefore help me to do my most effective work, would have the following characteristics (e.g., warm dry summers, skiing in the winter, a good newspaper, etc.):

1.

2.

3.

SPECIFIC
Working Conditions

At my place of work I could be happiest and do my most effective work, if I had the following working conditions (e.g., working indoors or out, not punching a timeclock, a boss who gave me free rein to do my work, having my own office, etc.):

1.

2.

3.

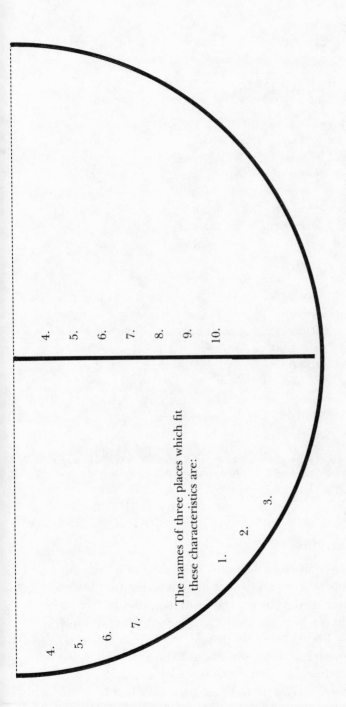

The names of three places which fit these characteristics are:

1.

2.

3.

4.

5.

6.

7.

4.

5.

6.

7.

8.

9.

10.

How to Prioritize Your Lists of Anything ••••••⋮•
(A Digression)

Here is a method for taking (say) ten items, and figuring out which one is most important to you, which is next most important, etc.

● Insert the items to be prioritized, in any order, in Section A. Then compare two items at a time, circling the one you prefer -- between the two -- in Section B. Which one is more important to you? State the question any way you want to: In the case of geographical factors, you might ask, "If I were being offered two jobs, one in an area that had factor #1, but not factor #2; the other in an area that had factor #2, but not factor #1, all other things being equal, which job would I take?" *Circle it.* Then go on to the next pair, etc.

● When you are all done, count up the number of times each number got circled, all told. Enter these totals on the TIMES line in Section C. Then notice the number of times each item was circled ("Times" = "Times Circled"). This determines the item's ranking. Most circled = #1, next most circled = #2, etc. Enter this ranking on the RANK line in Section C. If two items are circled the same number of times, look back in Section B to see -- when those two were compared there -- which one you preferred. Give that one an extra half point. List the items, now in their proper rank, in Section D.

Each time you use this grid, make a photocopy of it, and fill in the photocopy rather than the original. (You will need to photocopy this grid many times as you go through this map.)

Working Conditions

Now that you have filled out the General Geographical half of the Physical Settings petal, on to the other half: Working Conditions.

You use the same method as you did for Geography. In fact you can make up a chart where you copy the first four columns (only) of the Geography Chart. The only change you will need to make is to relabel column #1 as "Names of Places I Have Worked." Here name all the companies, or all the jobs you have ever held.

Column #2, now, is "Factors I Disliked and Still Dislike About That Job." Examples would be "no windows," "a boss that oversupervised me," "had to come in too early," etc.

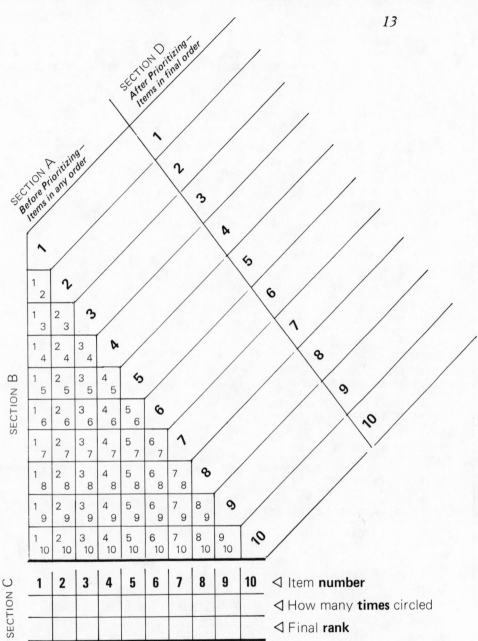

SECTION D
After Prioritizing—
Items in final order

SECTION A
Before Prioritizing—
Items in any order

SECTION B

SECTION C

| 1 | 2 | 3 | 4 | 5 | 6 | 7 | 8 | 9 | 10 |

◁ Item **number**
◁ How many **times** circled
◁ Final **rank**

Prioritizing Grid
for 10 Items

```
1  1  1  1  1  1  1  1  1  1  1  1  1  1  1  1  1  1  1  1  1  1  1
2  3  4  5  6  7  8  9  10 11 12 13 14 15 16 17 18 19 20 21 22 23 24

2  2  2  2  2  2  2  2  2  2  2  2  2  2  2  2  2  2  2  2  2  2
3  4  5  6  7  8  9  10 11 12 13 14 15 16 17 18 19 20 21 22 23 24

3  3  3  3  3  3  3  3  3  3  3  3  3  3  3  3  3  3  3  3  3
4  5  6  7  8  9  10 11 12 13 14 15 16 17 18 19 20 21 22 23 24

4  4  4  4  4  4  4  4  4  4  4  4  4  4  4  4  4  4  4  4
5  6  7  8  9  10 11 12 13 14 15 16 17 18 19 20 21 22 23 24

5  5  5  5  5  5  5  5  5  5  5  5  5  5  5  5  5  5  5
6  7  8  9  10 11 12 13 14 15 16 17 18 19 20 21 22 23 24

6  6  6  6  6  6  6  6  6  6  6  6  6  6  6  6  6  6
7  8  9  10 11 12 13 14 15 16 17 18 19 20 21 22 23 24

7  7  7  7  7  7  7  7  7  7  7  7  7  7  7  7  7
8  9  10 11 12 13 14 15 16 17 18 19 20 21 22 23 24

8  8  8  8  8  8  8  8  8  8  8  8  8  8  8  8
9  10 11 12 13 14 15 16 17 18 19 20 21 22 23 24

9  9  9  9  9  9  9  9  9  9  9  9  9  9  9
10 11 12 13 14 15 16 17 18 19 20 21 22 23 24

10 10 10 10 10 10 10 10 10 10 10 10 10 10
11 12 13 14 15 16 17 18 19 20 21 22 23 24

11 11 11 11 11 11 11 11 11 11 11 11 11
12 13 14 15 16 17 18 19 20 21 22 23 24

12 12 12 12 12 12 12 12 12 12 12 12
13 14 15 16 17 18 19 20 21 22 23 24

13 13 13 13 13 13 13 13 13 13 13
14 15 16 17 18 19 20 21 22 23 24

14 14 14 14 14 14 14 14 14 14
15 16 17 18 19 20 21 22 23 24

15 15 15 15 15 15 15 15 15
16 17 18 19 20 21 22 23 24

16 16 16 16 16 16 16 16
17 18 19 20 21 22 23 24

17 17 17 17 17 17 17
18 19 20 21 22 23 24

18 18 18 18 18 18
19 20 21 22 23 24

19 19 19 19 19
20 21 22 23 24

20 20 20 20
21 22 23 24

21 21 21
22 23 24

22 22
23 24

23
24
```

Total times each number got circled

1	2	3	4	5	6
7	8	9	10	11	12
13	14	15	16	17	18
19	20	21	22	23	24

Prioritizing Grid
for 24 Items

Each time you use this grid, make a photocopy of it, and fill in the photocopy rather than the original. (You will need to photocopy this grid many times as you go through this map.)

Columns #3 and #4 remain the same. List, and then prioritize, the positive factors about the working conditions you like best. Remember, these are also the working conditions under which you can do your best and most effective work. When you're done, list them on the right hand side of the petal on pages 10–11.

And voila! The first petal is all finished.

Step Two: Spiritual or Emotional Setting

Every job or career has not merely a physical setting, but a spiritual or emotional one also: the realm of things we cannot see. For example, a man once phoned me to ask what he should do about a crooked contract his firm had just executed. I asked him who drew it up. He said, "I did." I asked him why. He said, "My boss told me it was that, or I'd lose my job."

You need to think out, as part of your picture of your Ideal Job, what is important to you in life -- in the area of things we cannot see: values, principles, what you are willing to stand up for, and what you are not willing to stand up for, what you care about.

The most useful way to do this is to take a piece of blank paper (or two) and write out on it your *philosophy about life*: which typically might include some statement of why you think we are here on earth, what it is that you believe we are supposed to do while we are here, what you think is important in life and what is not important, and which values of our society you agree with, and which ones you disagree with. As a suggested framework only, you might want to choose from among these elements (you don't have to use them all):

- Behavior: how do you think we should behave in this world
- Beliefs: what are your strongest beliefs
- Choice: what do you think about its nature and importance
- Community: what ways do we belong to each other, and what do you think our responsibility is to each other
- Compassion: what do you think is its importance, and how should it be manifested in our daily life

The Second Petal

Spiritual or Emotional Setting I Like to Work In

MY PHILOSOPHY OF LIFE.

What I believe about life in general,
and my life in particular:
(key ideas here)

In order to do my best work,

these are the factors from my philosophy (above) that are especially important to me

to have at my work (or in my work):

- Confusion or ambivalence: how much do you think we need to learn to live with
- Death: what do you think about it and what do you think happens after it
- Events: what do you think makes things happen, and how do we explain this to ourselves
- Free will: what do you think: are things 'preordained to happen' or do we have free will
- God: see *Supreme Being*
- Heroes and heroines: who are yours
- Human: what do you think makes someone truly 'human'
- Love: what do you think is its nature and importance, along with all its related words: forgiveness, grace, etc.
- Principles: what ones are you willing to stand up for, which ones do you base your life on
- Purpose: why do you think we are here on earth, what do you think is the purpose of your life
- Reality: what comments do you have to make, about the nature of reality
- Sacrifice: what in life do you think is worth sacrificing for, and what kinds of sacrifice would you be willing to make
- Self: what do you believe about your self, ego, selfishness, selflessness
- Stewardship: what do you think we should do with God's gifts to us
- Supreme Being: do you have a concept of One, and if you do, what do you think the Supreme Being is like
- Values: what are the ones you hold most dear, sacred, and important

To help you in this latter area, you might want to examine your thoughts about the importance of *truth* (in what areas, particularly, does truth most matter to you?), the importance of *beauty* (what kinds of beauty do you like best?), *moral issues* (which ones are you most concerned about -- justice, feeding the hungry, helping the homeless, comforting AIDS sufferers, or what?), and the importance of *love*. Don't just *write*; take time also to *think!* Jot down the key ideas of your philosophy in the top part of the petal, on pages 16–17.

When you are done writing your philosophy of life, the bottom part of this petal asks you to lift out of that philosophy any factors which are especially important to you at your future place of work, or in your future work. For example, your philosophy of life might have reminded you: "I have to work in a place where I am never asked to do anything dishonest." Or: "I want to be among loving, supportive co-workers, and not among people who are always backbiting or gossiping about everyone." Whatever occurs to you, after studying your philosophy, put this stuff down, in the bottom part of that petal.

And, voila! The second petal is all finished.

Step Three: My Favorite Transferable Skills

Now, you know what it is you're going to do here. You are going to figure out what skills you use when you are enjoying yourself the most -- either in your work, or in your home, or when you are doing some hobby or recreation. These skills, no matter where you used them in the past, are transferable now to other jobs or careers.

There are two ways to identify your transferable skills: "Quick, but Superficial" and "Slow, but Absolutely Thorough." Let's look at "Quick, but Superficial" first.

The Party Exercise:
What Skills You Have and
Most Enjoy Using

As John L. Holland has taught us all, skills may be thought of as dividing into six clusters or families. To see which ones you are *attracted to*, try this exercise:

On the next page is an aerial view of a room in which a two-day (!) party is taking place. At this party, people with the same or similar interests have (for some reason) all gathered in the same corner of the room.

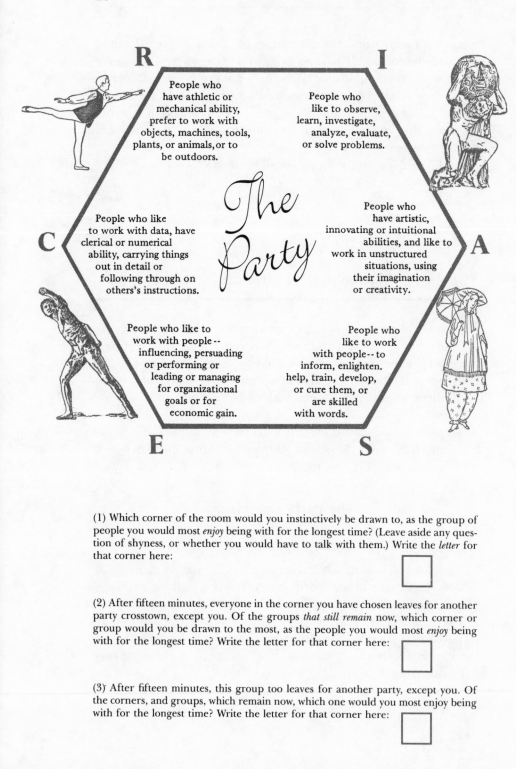

R

People who
have athletic or
mechanical ability,
prefer to work with
objects, machines, tools,
plants, or animals, or to
be outdoors.

I

People who
like to observe,
learn, investigate,
analyze, evaluate,
or solve problems.

The Party

C

People who like
to work with data, have
clerical or numerical
ability, carrying things
out in detail or
following through on
others's instructions.

A

People who
have artistic,
innovating or intuitional
abilities, and like to
work in unstructured
situations, using
their imagination
or creativity.

E

People who like to
work with people --
influencing, persuading
or performing or
leading or managing
for organizational
goals or for
economic gain.

S

People who
like to work
with people -- to
inform, enlighten.
help, train, develop,
or cure them, or
are skilled
with words.

(1) Which corner of the room would you instinctively be drawn to, as the group of people you would most *enjoy* being with for the longest time? (Leave aside any question of shyness, or whether you would have to talk with them.) Write the *letter* for that corner here:

(2) After fifteen minutes, everyone in the corner you have chosen leaves for another party crosstown, except you. Of the groups *that still remain* now, which corner or group would you be drawn to the most, as the people you would most *enjoy* being with for the longest time? Write the letter for that corner here:

(3) After fifteen minutes, this group too leaves for another party, except you. Of the corners, and groups, which remain now, which one would you most enjoy being with for the longest time? Write the letter for that corner here:

*(If you want to explore this further, see Holland, John L., "Self-Directed Search, 1985 Revision." This is a self-marking test which you can use to discover your "Holland code" and what occupations you might **start** your research with. You can order an SDS Specimen Set for less than $5, which includes the SDS, a brief Occupations Finder, and a booklet, "You and Your Career," from the publisher, Psychological Assessment Resources, Inc., Box 998, Odessa, FL 33556.)*

Now, on to "Slow, but Absolutely Thorough."

In order to find out this information, it will be necessary for you to write out seven (7) stories of some enjoyable and satisfying experiences or accomplishments which you have done in your life. Which stories should you choose? Ah, that's a good question. Not necessarily the ones which occur to you right off the top of your head. Sometimes you have to dig deeper.

To guard yourself against impulsively choosing stories which may not tell you much about your skills, it is helpful to construct a basic outline of your life, for yourself, first. One way to do this is through a Memory Net.

The Memory Net

That Net is on the next page. You should take at least three hours (with some hard thinking, as well as writing) to fill it in.

In the first column of the Memory Net are the years of your life, divided into five-year periods (cross out the years before your birth, of course). Some of you will be able to remember what activities you were doing during each of these five-year periods, just from seeing the dates. Use this column, then, to jog your memory, and fill in the rest of the Net.

The second column is for those of you who don't remember things by Dates, but by what job you were holding down (or what school you were attending). Use this column, then, to jog your memory -- fill it in, and then fill in the rest of the Net.

The third column is for those of you who don't remember things by either Years or Jobs, but by where you were living at the time. Use this column, then, to jog your memory -- fill it in, and then fill in the rest of the Net.

Once you've tackled the first three columns, as you go across the rest of the Memory Net you will generally find it pays to fill in the three Activities columns first (columns 4, 6, and 8), and then go back to the Accomplishments columns (5, 7, and 9). That is to say, once you remember what you were doing (activities) in the way of

Memory

| Column 1 | Column 2 | Column 3 | Column 4 | Column 5 |

Jogging Your Memory   Leisure

In Terms of Five-Year Periods	In Terms of Jobs You Have Held	In Terms of Places You Have Lived	Activities	Accomplishments
e.g. 1985–1989				
1980–1984				
1975–1979				
1970–1974				
1965–1969				
1960–1964				
1955–1959				
1950–1954				
1945–1949				
1940–1944				
1935–1939				
1930–1934				
1925–1929				
1920–1924				
1915–1919				

Column 6	*Column 7*	*Column 8*	*Column 9*

Learning   Labor

Activities	Accomplishments	Activities	Accomplishments

Leisure, Learning, or Labor (Work), you will then find it easier to think of specific accomplishments in your Leisure or your Learning or your Labor. Put down titles only, or a few words to jog your memory, rather than attempting any more detailed description of your accomplishments, at this time.

Once you have the Net all filled in, you are ready to choose and write your stories. You will need at least seven blank sheets of paper. On each of these sheets you are (eventually) going to write one of your stories -- picked from the Memory Net. Then you will analyze each story, one by one, to see what skills you were using, in that story.

For the time being, you start by writing **just one** of those stories. Look over your Memory Net, and most particularly at columns 5, 7, and 9. Look at your accomplishments. Whether they were early in your life, or more recently, whether they were in your leisure life, or your learning life, or your labor/work life, does not matter.

Just be sure also that it deals in turn with TASK, TOOLS, AND MEANS, and OUTCOME or RESULT. See the example that follows here.

---

1. A TASK. Something you wanted to do, just because it was fun or would give you a sense of adventure or a sense of accomplishment. Normally there was a problem that you were trying to solve, or a challenge you were trying to overcome, or something you were trying to master or produce or create.

2. TOOLS OR MEANS. You used something to help you do the task, solve the problem, overcome the challenge. Either you had certain *Things* to help you -- objects, materials, tools or equipment, or you had other *People* to help you, or you got a hold of some vital *Information*. Tell us what tools or means you used, and how you used them.

3. AN OUTCOME OR RESULT. You were able to finish the task or solve the problem, overcome the challenge, master a process, or produce or create something. You had a sense of pride, even if no one else knew what it was you had accomplished.[1]

---

1. © *Copyright 1988 by D. Porot. Adapted and used by his permission.*

Once you have selected your first story, write it out in detail --
but keep it comparatively brief -- two or three paragraphs at most.
Be sure that it is *a story* you tell -- that is, that it moves step by step.
It may help if you pretend that you are telling it to a small whining
child who keeps saying, "An' then whadja do?" "An' then whadja
do?"

When you are done, label that sheet "#1".

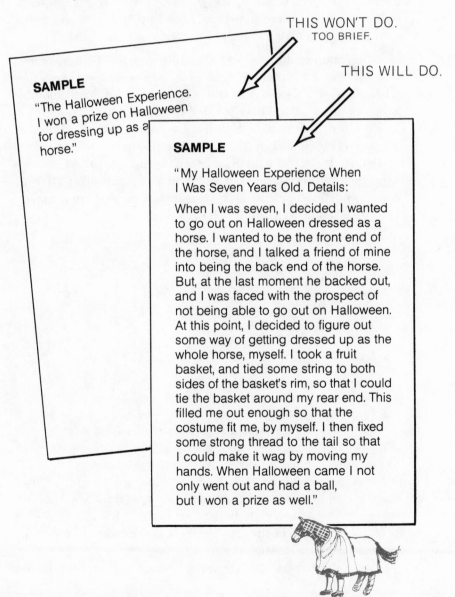

THIS WON'T DO.
TOO BRIEF.

THIS WILL DO.

SAMPLE

"The Halloween Experience.
I won a prize on Halloween
for dressing up as a
horse."

SAMPLE

"My Halloween Experience When
I Was Seven Years Old. Details:

When I was seven, I decided I wanted
to go out on Halloween dressed as a
horse. I wanted to be the front end of
the horse, and I talked a friend of mine
into being the back end of the horse.
But, at the last moment he backed out,
and I was faced with the prospect of
not being able to go out on Halloween.
At this point, I decided to figure out
some way of getting dressed up as the
whole horse, myself. I took a fruit
basket, and tied some string to both
sides of the basket's rim, so that I could
tie the basket around my rear end. This
filled me out enough so that the
costume fit me, by myself. I then fixed
some strong thread to the tail so that
I could make it wag by moving my
hands. When Halloween came I not
only went out and had a ball,
but I won a prize as well."

Identifying Your Skills

Once this first story is written, you are ready to identify what skills you used, in that story. The list of skills you are to use is found on pages 28-33. The skills resemble a series of typewriter keys. You go down each column vertically. As you look at each key, you ask yourself, "Did I use this skill **in this story**? (story #1)." If you did, you color in the little box *right under* that key which has the number 1 in it (color right *over* the "1"). We suggest you use a **red** pen, pencil, or crayon, to do this coloring in. Keep going down each column, in turn, on each of the following six pages.

When you are done with all the skills keys, for Things, People, and Information, you have finished with story #1. You now know what skills you used while you were doing this first enjoyable achievement, that you have selected to analyze.

However, "one swallow doth not a summer make," and the fact you used certain skills in this one accomplishment doesn't yet tell you much. What you want to look for are patterns: i.e., which skills keep getting used, again and again, in accomplishment after accomplishment, story after story. It is *the patterns* that are meaningful for choosing your future job or career.

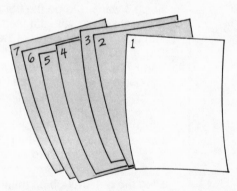

So now it is time to take a second sheet of paper, label it "#2", and look over the Memory Net to see which achievement you want to pick for your second story. Once you have written it out in detail, you go back to the Skills Keys and again ask yourself, "Did I use this skill **in this story**? (story #2)." And, again, if you did, you color in the little box right under that key that has the number 2 in it (color right over the "2"). Again, use the red pen, pencil, or crayon. Continue through the six Skill pages.

Take a third sheet and repeat the process, and so, continue on through sheet (and story) #7. When you are done, look over the Skills pages to see which skills stand out (i.e., which ones have the little boxes under them colored in the most).

Choosing Your Favorite Transferable Skills

You must now choose your favorites, from the Skills pages you just filled out. How you make that choice is entirely up to you. Here are two different methods for doing this:

a) **The Top Ten**. Look at all the Skills pages you just filled out, and put a big check mark by your ten favorite skills -- never mind whether they are with Things, People, or Information. It could turn out, for example, that eight of your favorite skills are with Things, and one with People and one with Information. On a sheet of scratch paper, list all ten and then rearrange them so that they end up being listed *in their order of importance for you*. You can do this prioritizing either by guess and by gosh, **or** by using the Prioritizing Grid on page 13. What you want to end up with is a *prioritized list* -- on which the skill that is most important to you is listed first, the skill that is next most important to you is listed second, next most important is third, next most important is fourth, and so on. Copy these onto page 35.

b) Alternative Method: **Eight, Eight, and Eight**. Look at the Skills pages and pick your eight favorites off *each diagram*: your eight favorite Skills with Things, your eight favorite Skills with People, and your eight favorite Skills with Information. Put *each* eight in order, again either by guessing, or by using the Prioritizing Grid three times. You will end up with three lists: your eight favorite Skills with Things, *in order of priority for you*; and your eight favorite Skills with People, *in order of priority for you*; and your eight favorite Skills with Information, *in order of priority for you*. Copy these onto page 36-37.

Optional: Restating Skills in Your Own Language

Now (and only now) that you have a list of your favorite skills -- either The Top Ten or the Eight, Eight, and Eight -- you *may* want to restate them in other language than was on the Skills diagrams, language that is more uniquely and personally yours. *If so,*

(continued on page 34)

28

My transferable skills dealing with

THINGS

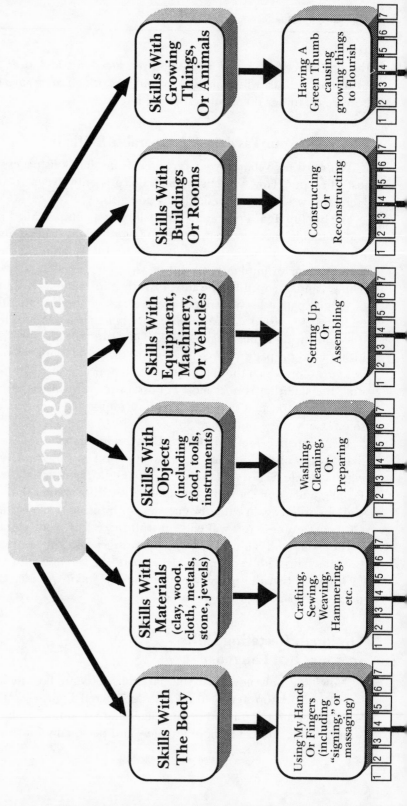

I am good at

Skills With Growing Things, Or Animals
→ Having A Green Thumb causing growing things to flourish
1 2 3 4 5 6 7

Skills With Buildings Or Rooms
→ Constructing Or Reconstructing
1 2 3 4 5 6 7

Skills With Equipment, Machinery, Or Vehicles
→ Setting Up, Or Assembling
1 2 3 4 5 6 7

Skills With Objects (including food, tools, instruments)
→ Washing, Cleaning, Or Preparing
1 2 3 4 5 6 7

Skills With Materials (clay, wood, cloth, metals, stone, jewels)
→ Crafting, Sewing, Weaving, Hammering, etc.
1 2 3 4 5 6 7

Skills With The Body
→ Using My Hands Or Fingers (including "signing," or massaging)
1 2 3 4 5 6 7

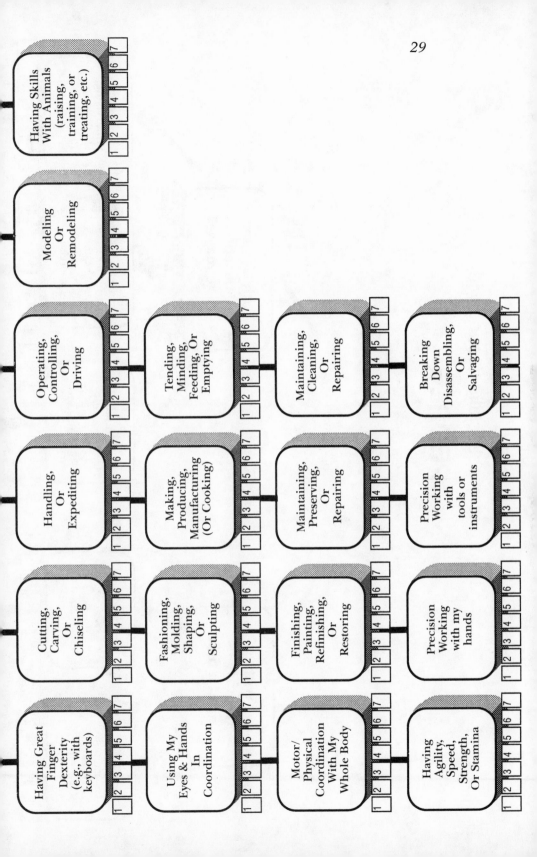

My transferable skills dealing with

PEOPLE

I am good at

With Groups, Organizations, or the masses

Managing, Supervising, Or Running (a business, fund drive, etc.)
1 2 3 4 5 6 7

Playing Games, or a particular game, Leading Others in recreation or exercise
1 2 3 4 5 6 7

Communicating Effectively to a group or a multitude
1 2 3 4 5 6 7

With Individuals one at a time

Diagnosing, Treating, Or Healing
1 2 3 4 5 6 7

Taking Instructions, Serving, Or Helping
1 2 3 4 5 6 7

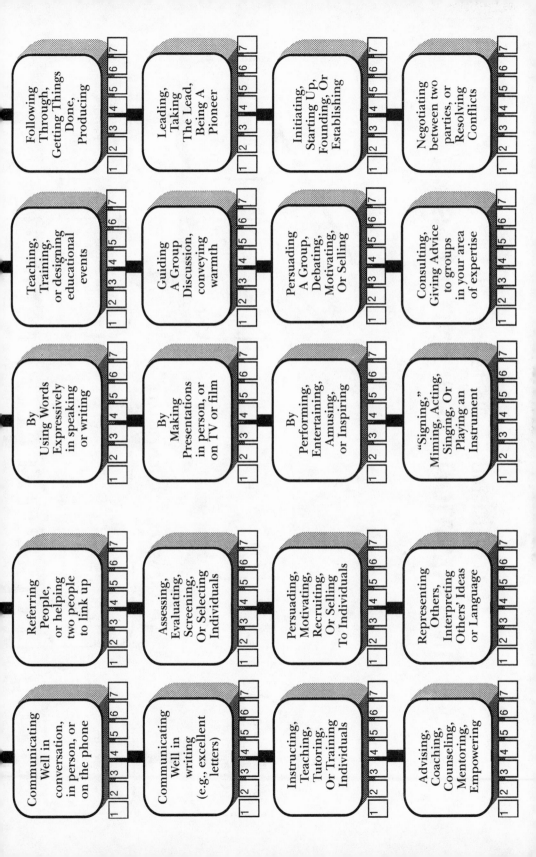

32

My transferable skills dealing with

INFORMATION, DATA, AND IDEAS

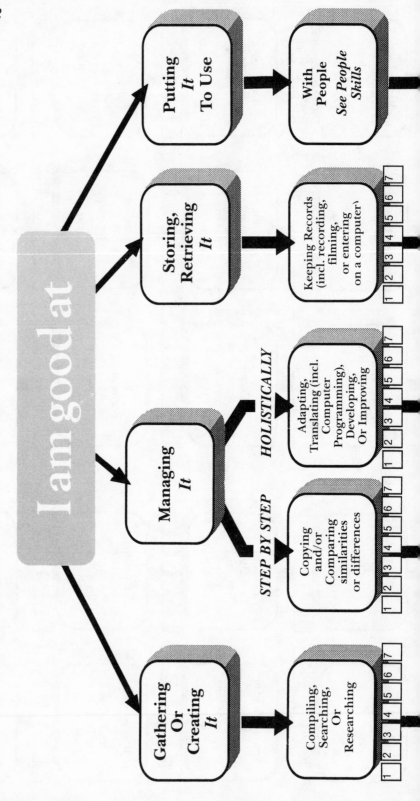

I am good at

Putting *It* To Use → **With People** *See People Skills*

Storing, Retrieving *It* → **Keeping Records** (incl. recording, filming, or entering on a computer)
1 2 3 4 5 6 7

Managing *It*

HOLISTICALLY → **Adapting, Translating (incl. Computer Programming), Developing, Or Improving**
1 2 3 4 5 6 7

STEP BY STEP → **Copying and/or Comparing similarities or differences**
1 2 3 4 5 6 7

Gathering Or Creating *It* → **Compiling, Searching, Or Researching**
1 2 3 4 5 6 7

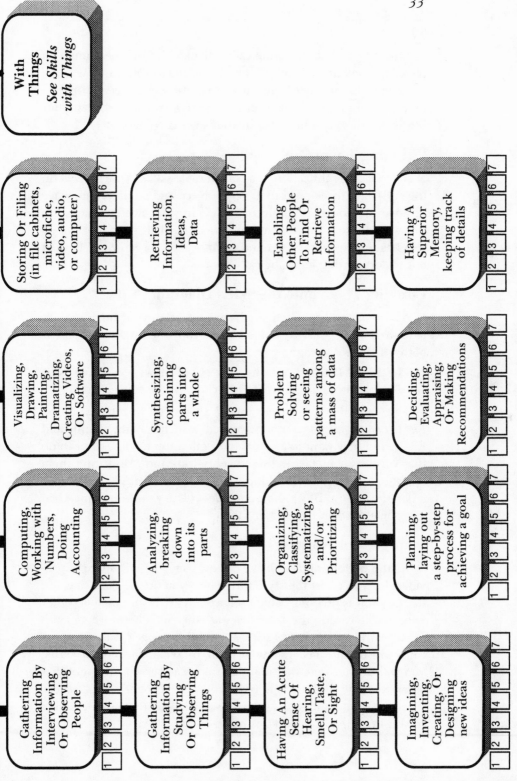

With Things
See Skills with Things

Storing Or Filing (in file cabinets, microfiche, video, audio, or computer)
1 2 3 4 5 6 7

Retrieving Information, Ideas, Data
1 2 3 4 5 6 7

Enabling Other People To Find Or Retrieve Information
1 2 3 4 5 6 7

Having A Superior Memory, keeping track of details
1 2 3 4 5 6 7

Visualizing, Drawing, Painting, Dramatizing, Creating Videos, Or Software
1 2 3 4 5 6 7

Synthesizing, combining parts into a whole
1 2 3 4 5 6 7

Problem Solving or seeing patterns among a mass of data
1 2 3 4 5 6 7

Deciding, Evaluating, Appraising, Or Making Recommendations
1 2 3 4 5 6 7

Computing, Working with Numbers, Doing Accounting
1 2 3 4 5 6 7

Analyzing, breaking down into its parts
1 2 3 4 5 6 7

Organizing, Classifying, Systematizing, and/or Prioritizing
1 2 3 4 5 6 7

Planning, laying out a step-by-step process for achieving a goal
1 2 3 4 5 6 7

Gathering Information By Interviewing Or Observing People
1 2 3 4 5 6 7

Gathering Information By Studying Or Observing Things
1 2 3 4 5 6 7

Having An Acute Sense Of Hearing, Smell, Taste, Or Sight
1 2 3 4 5 6 7

Imagining, Inventing, Creating, Or Designing new ideas
1 2 3 4 5 6 7

turn to the vocabulary section called "Uniquely You," beginning on page 72. Look up the skills which you picked as your favorites, and see if you prefer any of the words that are offered as alternatives there. You can, of course, rephrase even *these* words, so that your list, in the end, is completely in your own language.

'Fleshing Them Out'

A *complete* identification of a transferable skill of yours *should* (in the end) have three parts to it: verb, object, and modifier (adjective or adverb). Now that you have *the verb* in your own language you *may* want to flesh out each of your favorite skills so that each one also has some general *object* and *modifier*, e.g., "organizing" fleshed out to "organizing ideas logically."

Copying Them onto the Skills Diagram

As we said earlier, when you have your list of your favorite skills in a final form that is satisfying to you, copy the list onto either (or both) of these diagrams:

The Block Diagram, on the next page, allows you to put your *Top Ten* favorite skills, in order of priority.

The Tasks Petal on pages 36–37 allows you to list your *Eight, Eight, and Eight.* (If you *only* worked with the Eight, Eight, and Eight, and now want to also hammer out a top ten list, you can do that very easily by taking these twenty-four and prioritizing them together -- listing the resulting top ten of the twenty-four, *in order of priority*, on the Block diagram below.) Use the Prioritizing Grid if you need to, on page 14.

Your *Style* of Working

At the bottom of *The Tasks Petal* on pages 36–37, space is provided for you to list **the style** with which you do the skills that you do. Often it is this style which sets you apart from nineteen other people who can do the same tasks as you can. Therefore, *this part of the exercise should not be skipped over.* Following is a list of styles (they are often called **personal traits** or **self-management skills**; you will further note that many of them can serve as the **modifier** when you are fleshing out your skill verbs, above). Put a check mark in front of any word (or phrase) below that you think applies to you in your work. Add any others that occur to you, which are

(continued on page 38)

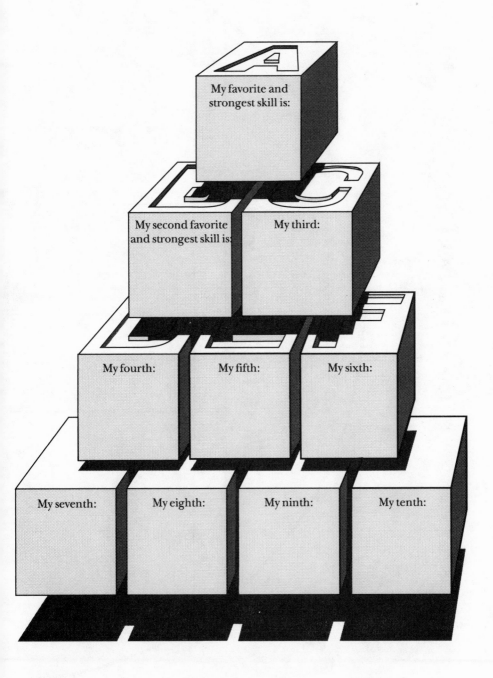

36

The Third Petal

Tasks

In order to do my favorite Tasks,
I need to be using my favorite
Functional/Transferable Skills.
These are:

What I Like to Do With

THINGS	PEOPLE	INFORMATION
1.	1.	1.
2.	2.	2.
3.	3.	3.
4.	4.	4.

5.

6.

7.

8.

5.

6.

7.

8.

5.

6.

7.

8.

My Style
of Doing Them:

(so-called "traits" or "self-management skills")
e.g., "quickly," "thoroughly," "painstakingly," etc.

not on this list. Then when you are done checking, pick the ten that you think are **most** important, and copy them onto the bottom part of *The Tasks Petal -- in their order of importance to you, if you can.* This matter of *importance* will most often come down to a question of which style you are proudest of, next proudest of, and so forth. Use the Prioritizing Grid if you need to (on page 14).

Style with Which I Do These Skills

• I am VERY:

- ☐ Accurate
- ☐ Achievement-oriented
- ☐ Adaptable
- ☐ Adept
- ☐ Adept at having fun
- ☐ Adventuresome
- ☐ Alert
- ☐ Appreciative
- ☐ Assertive
- ☐ Astute
- ☐ Authoritative
- ☐ Calm
- ☐ Cautious
- ☐ Charismatic
- ☐ Competent
- ☐ Consistent
- ☐ Contagious in my enthusiasm
- ☐ Cooperative
- ☐ Courageous
- ☐ Creative
- ☐ Decisive
- ☐ Deliberate
- ☐ Dependable/have dependability
- ☐ Diligent
- ☐ Diplomatic
- ☐ Discreet

- ☐ Driving
- ☐ Dynamic
- ☐ Extremely economical
- ☐ Effective
- ☐ Energetic
- ☐ Enthusiastic
- ☐ Exceptional
- ☐ Exhaustive
- ☐ Experienced
- ☐ Expert
- ☐ Firm
- ☐ Flexible
- ☐ Humanly oriented
- ☐ Impulsive
- ☐ Independent
- ☐ Innovative
- ☐ Knowledgeable
- ☐ Loyal
- ☐ Methodical
- ☐ Objective
- ☐ Open-minded
- ☐ Outgoing
- ☐ Outstanding
- ☐ Patient
- ☐ Penetrating
- ☐ Perceptive
- ☐ Persevering
- ☐ Persistent

- ☐ Pioneering
- ☐ Practical
- ☐ Professional
- ☐ Protective
- ☐ Punctual
- ☐ Quick/work quickly
- ☐ Rational
- ☐ Realistic
- ☐ Reliable
- ☐ Repeatedly
- ☐ Resourceful
- ☐ Responsible
- ☐ Responsive
- ☐ Safeguarding
- ☐ Self-motivated
- ☐ Self-reliant
- ☐ Sensitive
- ☐ Sophisticated, very sophisticated
- ☐ Strong
- ☐ Supportive
- ☐ Tactful
- ☐ Thorough
- ☐ Unique
- ☐ Unusual
- ☐ Versatile
- ☐ Vigorous

• I am a person who:

With respect to execution of a task, and achievement

- ☐ Takes initiative
- ☐ Is able to handle a great variety of tasks and responsibilities simultaneously and efficiently

☐ Takes risks
☐   Takes calculated risks
☐ Is expert at getting things done

With respect to time, and achievement

☐ Consistently tackles tasks ahead of time
☐ Is adept at finding ways to speed up a task
☐ Gets the most done in the shortest time
☐ Expedites the task at hand
☐ Meets deadlines
☐   Delivers on promises on time
☐   Brings projects in on time and within budget

With respect to working conditions

☐ Maintains order and neatness in my workspace
☐ Is attendant to details
☐ Has a high tolerance of repetition and/or monotonous routines
☐ Likes planning and directing an entire activity
☐ Demonstrates mastery
☐ Promotes change
☐ Works well under pressure and still improvises
☐ Enjoys a challenge
☐ Loves working outdoors
☐ Loves to travel
☐ Has an unusually good grasp of . . .
☐ Is good at responding to emergencies
☐ Has the courage of his or her convictions

When you are done with this exercise, copy the results at the bottom of the Tasks petal. You are now ready to move on.

The Things You Like to Act Upon

These next three steps, and the next three petals as a matter of fact, are called "**Tools or Means.**" Skills *always* require some tool or means. A tool or means is something you love **to handle**, or something you like **to use**, or something you like **to work on**, or **act upon**. It may be *people*, or *information*, or a *thing*.

For example, if you love to hammer things, you need both a hammer and a thing to hammer -- let us say a nail. The hammer and the nail are the tools or means that enable you to use your skill -- of hammering. And, in this case, they are *things*. Of course, you also need some knowledge of *how to hammer*, and that means that some *information* is also used here, as a tool or means.

On the succeeding three petals, and in the succeeding three steps, we will look first at People, and then at Information, and then at Things, to see which of these are your favorites.

Step Four: My Favorite People to Work With

If you checked any skills with People, as your favorites, in Step Three, it is important that you now specify *what kind* of People you prefer to work with. Let us say, for example, that you checked "teaching" as one of your favorite skills. The question now is: *What* people do you most enjoy teaching? All people? Particular age groups? If so, which ones? People with particular problems? If so, which ones? People who are working on particular issues in their life? If so, which ones?

Following is a list of people. Put a check mark in front of any description that describes people you particularly like (or think you would particularly like) to work with -- as clients, customers, students, or whatever, in your work. Add any others that may occur to you, which are not on the list. Then when you are done checking, pick the ten that you think are **most** important, and copy them onto the Petal called *Tools or Means: 1* (found on pages 44–45) -- *in your order of preference. "I would most enjoy working with these people, next with these people, next with these people,"* etc. Use the Prioritizing Grid if you need to (on page 14).

Kinds of People I Prefer to Serve Or Try to Help

- ☐ Men
- ☐ Women
- ☐ Individuals
- ☐ Groups of eight or less
- ☐ Groups larger than eight
- ☐ Babies
- ☐ School-age children
- ☐ Adolescents or young people
- ☐ College students
- ☐ Young adults
- ☐ People in their thirties
- ☐ The middle-aged
- ☐ The elderly
- ☐ The retired
- ☐ All people regardless of age
- ☐ Heterosexuals
- ☐ Homosexuals
- ☐ All people regardless of sex
- ☐ People of a particular cultural background
- ☐ People of a particular economic background
- ☐ People of a particular social background
- ☐ People of a particular educational background
- ☐ People of a particular philosophy or religious belief:
- ☐ Certain kinds of workers (blue-collar, white-collar, executives, or whatever):
- ☐ People who are poor:
- ☐ People who are powerless:
- ☐ People who wield power:
- ☐ People who are rich:
- ☐ People who are easy to work with:
- ☐ People who are difficult to work with:
- ☐ People in a particular place (the Armed Forces, prison, etc.)

Kinds of Problems I Like to Try to Help People With:

- ☐ Physical handicaps
- ☐ Overweight
- ☐ Mental retardation
- ☐ Pain
- ☐ Disease in general
- ☐ Hypertension
- ☐ Allergies
- ☐ Self-healing, psychic healing
- ☐ Terminal illness
- ☐ Holistic health
- ☐ Life/work planning or adjustment
- ☐ Identifying and finding meaningful work
- ☐ Job-hunting, career change, unemployment, being fired or laid off
- ☐ Illiteracy, educational needs
- ☐ Industry in-house training
- ☐ Performance problems, appraisal
- ☐ Low energy
- ☐ Nutritional problems
- ☐ Physical fitness
- ☐ Work satisfaction
- ☐ Discipline problems, self-discipline
- ☐ Stress
- ☐ Sleep disorders
- ☐ Relationships
- ☐ Personal insight, therapy
- ☐ Loneliness
- ☐ Boredom
- ☐ Complaints, grievances
- ☐ Anger
- ☐ Anxiety
- ☐ Fear
- ☐ Shyness
- ☐ Meeting people, starting friendships

- ☐ Communications, thoughts, feelings
- ☐ Love
- ☐ Self-acceptance and acceptance of others
- ☐ Learning how to love
- ☐ Marriage
- ☐ Competing needs
- ☐ Sexual education, sexual problems
- ☐ Sexual dysfunction
- ☐ Pregnancy and childbirth
- ☐ Parenting
- ☐ Physical abuse
- ☐ Rape
- ☐ Divorce
- ☐ Death and grief

- ☐ Addictions
- ☐ Drug problems
- ☐ Alcoholism
- ☐ Smoking
- ☐ Mental illness
- ☐ Depression
- ☐ Psychiatric hospitalization
- ☐ Personal economics
- ☐ Financial planning
- ☐ Possessions
- ☐ Budgeting
- ☐ Debt bankruptcy
- ☐ Values
- ☐ Ethics
- ☐ Philosophy or religion
- ☐ Worship
- ☐ Stewardship
- ☐ Life after death
- ☐ Psychic phenomena

If while you are checking off these descriptions, you see any which apply to the kind of **co-workers** you would most like to have, copy them onto the bottom part of the same petal. (You may also find clues about your preferred co-workers, in *the Styles list* that you worked on in the previous exercise.) The following list may also help. Check off the descriptions which apply, or add any others which occur to you:

My Preferred Co-workers:

I prefer to work with what kinds of co-workers or colleagues, bosses, or subordinates?

- ☐ Both sexes
- ☐ Men primarily
- ☐ Women primarily
- ☐ People of all ages
- ☐ Adolescents or young people
- ☐ College students
- ☐ Young adults
- ☐ People in their thirties
- ☐ The middle-aged
- ☐ The elderly
- ☐ The retired
- ☐ All people regardless of sexual orientation
- ☐ Heterosexuals
- ☐ Homosexuals

- [ ] All people regardless of background
- [ ]   People of a particular background:
- [ ]   People of a particular cultural background:
- [ ]   People of a particular economic background:
- [ ]   People of a particular social background:
- [ ]   People of a particular educational background:
- [ ]   People of a particular philosophy or religious belief:
- [ ]   Certain kinds of workers (blue-collar, white-collar, executives, or whatever):
- [ ]   People in a particular place (the Armed Forces, prison, etc.):
- [ ] People who are easy to work with:
- [ ] People who are difficult to work with:

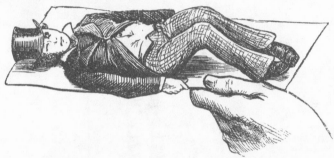

In the bottom part of this same Petal, on page 45 you will see an outline of a hexagon. This represents the Party Exercise, found on page 20, and is put there to remind you that you *may* want to put down *the descriptions* from your *favorite* corners of the hexagon, as descriptions of what you would like your co-workers to be doing (true, the corners you chose were supposed to be descriptive of *you*, but in identifying co-workers you would like to work with, the ancient truth is that birds of a feather tend to like to flock to-gether -- e.g., artistic types tend to like to work and communicate with other artistic types, not accountants in three-piece suits -- and vice versa). Within the hexagon on that petal, you will see a figure resembling a cross -- to remind you (you are at the center of the figure) to think out what kind of person you want *over* you as boss (top of the figure), *beside* you as co-workers (middle of the figure) and *below* you, as subordinates (bottom of the figure).

When you are all done with this exercise, you will have now fin-ished the fourth petal out of eight; the picture of your ideal job should be starting to get clearer. Also you can begin to see how you are cutting down the size of the job-market that you will need to explore, to a much more manageable territory. On to the next step.

The Fourth Petal

Tools or Means: 1

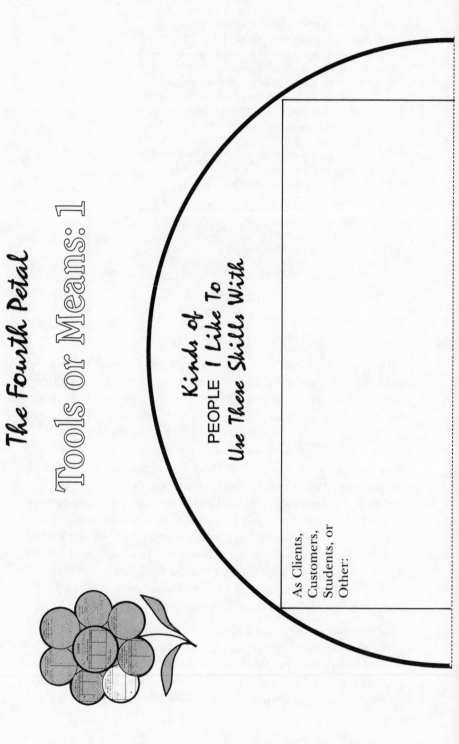

Kinds of
PEOPLE I Like To
Use These Skills With

As Clients,
Customers,
Students, or
Other:

As Co-workers:

Step Five: My Favorite Kinds Of Information That I Like To Work With

If you checked any skills with Information, as your favorites, in Step Three, it is important that you now specify *what kind* of Information you prefer to work with. This will break down, as you can see from the next petal, on pages 48–49 to **Form** and **Content**.

Form is a matter of: Do you prefer to work with information in the form of newspapers, magazines, books, computer output, reports, pictures, or what?

Following is a more complete list of such forms. Put a check mark in front of any word (or phrase) below that describes forms of information you enjoy (or think you would enjoy) working with at your place of work. Add any others that occur to you, which are not on this list. Then when you are done checking, pick the ten that you think are **most** important to you, and copy them onto the left hand side of the petal called *Tools or Means: 2 (pages 48–49) -- in their order of importance to you, if you can. Use the Prioritizing Grid if you need to on page 14).*

Forms of Information I Prefer to Work with, or Help Produce:

☐ Books
☐ Magazines
☐ Newspapers
☐ Catalogs
☐ Handbooks
☐ Records, files
☐ Trade or professional literature
☐ Videotapes
☐ Audiotapes
☐ Computer printouts
☐ Seminars, learning from trainers
☐ Courses, learning from teachers

☐ Words
☐ Numbers or statistics
☐ Specifications
☐ Precision requirements
☐ Statistical analyses
☐ Data analysis studies
☐ Financial needs
☐ Costs
☐ Accountings
☐ Symbols
☐ Designs
☐ Blueprints
☐ Wall-charts

- ☐   Time-charts
- ☐   Schema
- ☐ Facts
- ☐   History
- ☐ Ideas
- ☐   Conceptions
- ☐ Investigations
- ☐ Opinion-collection
- ☐   Points of view
- ☐   Surveys

- ☐ Research projects, research and development projects, project reports
- ☐ Procedures
- ☐ Guidebooks
- ☐ Manuals

I Like to Collect or Deal with Information about Any of the Following:

- ☐ Principles
- ☐   Physical principles
- ☐   Spiritual principles
- ☐ Values
- ☐ Standards
- ☐   Repeating requirements
- ☐   Variables
- ☐ Frameworks
- ☐   Organizational contexts
- ☐   Boundary conditions
- ☐   Parameters
- ☐ Systems

- ☐ Programs
- ☐ Operations
- ☐ Sequences
- ☐ Methods
- ☐   Techniques
- ☐   Procedures
- ☐   Specialized procedures
- ☐ Analyses
- ☐   Data analysis studies
- ☐   Schematic analyses
- ☐   Intuitions

I Like to Help Put Information to Use in Any of the Following Practical Ways:

- ☐ Principles applications
- ☐ Recommendations
- ☐   Policy recommendations
- ☐ Goals
- ☐   Project goals
- ☐ Objectives
- ☐ Solutions
- ☐   New approaches

- ☐ Plans
- ☐   Tactical needs
- ☐ Performance characteristics
- ☐   Proficiencies
- ☐   Deficiencies
- ☐   Reporting systems
- ☐   Controls systems

(continued on page 50)

The Fifth Petal

Tools or Means: 2

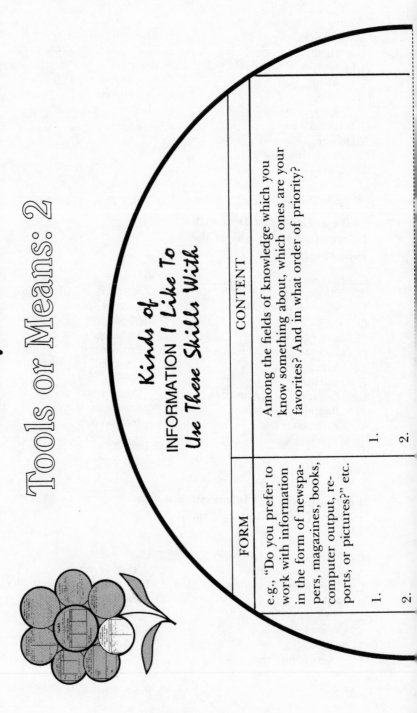

Kinds of INFORMATION I Like To Use These Skills With

FORM

e.g., "Do you prefer to work with information in the form of newspapers, magazines, books, computer output, reports, or pictures?" etc.

1.

2.

CONTENT

Among the fields of knowledge which you know something about, which ones are your favorites? And in what order of priority?

1.

2.

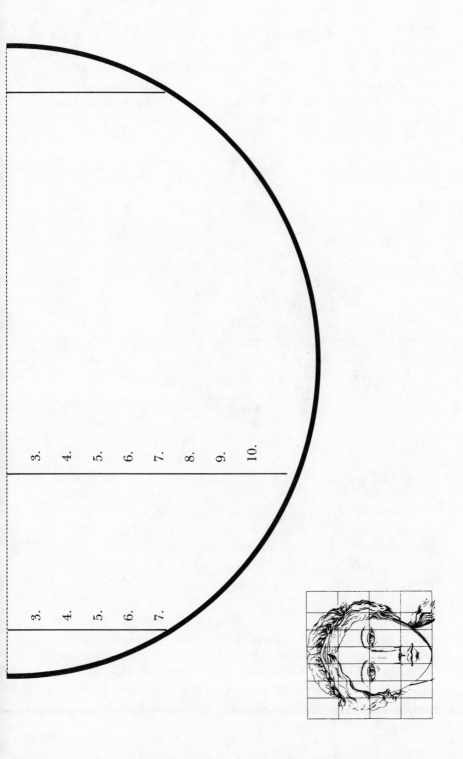

3. 4. 5. 6. 7. 8. 9. 10.

3. 4. 5. 6. 7.

If this checklist doesn't seem relevant to your life, don't worry about it. It helps some people (a lot), while it leaves others cold. Anyway, one way or another, when you are done with this checklist, and have listed your top seven on the left hand side of the petal on pages 48–49, then it is time to turn from **Form** to **Content**. Content is on the right hand side of that same petal.

Content is a matter of: Among the fields that you know something about, which ones are your favorites? Do you love the knowledge you have about computers, or the knowledge you have about the Environment, or your knowledge of antiques, or gardening, or skiing, or painting, or psychology, or the Bible -- or what?

A field is always a *subject*, or a *major* (as in college), or "*Principles of . . .*," or "*How to . . .*," or "*Rules of . . .*," or "*The Secrets of . . .*," etc.

Generally speaking, you picked up such knowledge in four different ways (at least), and these four ways form a handy chart for recalling to yourself what are the fields you know something about.

You want to list *all* the fields you know anything about, this first time 'round, whether you **like** them or not. You can go back later and check off your favorites, as well as cross out the ones you just hate.

Fields of Knowledge That You Learned About

In School or College (At Home or Work)	On the Job, or Just by Doing (At Home or Work)	From Seminars or Workshops	By Personal Instruction from People or by Reading a Lot

Here are some *examples* to guide you in filling in the chart:

Fields of Knowledge I Learned About in School or College

e.g., Spanish
Psychology
Biology
Geometry
Accounting
Music appreciation
Typing
Sociology

(continued on next page)

**Fields of Knowledge I Learned About on the Job, or
Just by Doing (at Home or Work)**

*e.g., How to operate a computer
How a volunteer organization works
Principles of planning and management*

Fields of Knowledge I Learned from Seminars or Workshops

*e.g., The way the brain works
Principles of art
Speed reading
Drawing*

**Fields of Knowledge I Learned About by Personal Instruction
from People or by Reading a Lot**

*e.g., How to sew
How to drive an automobile
How computers work
Principles of comparison shopping
Knowledge of antiques
Principles of outdoor survival*

You may want to look back at your Memory Net, pages 22–
23, at this point, for help in filling in the preceding chart. *And*,
to further aid you, you may want to see a list, or at least a sampler,
of other possible fields of knowledge, just to jog your memory. Following is such a list. Put a check mark in front of any word (or
phrase) that describes possible fields of knowledge that you already
are familiar with, and would enjoy getting a chance to use in your
ideal job. Write in any others that occur to you, as you go down
this list.

*A SAMPLER OF POSSIBLE FIELDS
YOU MAY KNOW ABOUT*

Primarily about People

☐ Sociology
☐ The *how to* of customer
relations and service
☐ Principles of group dynamics
☐ Principles of behavioral
modification
☐ Instructional principles and
techniques

☐ Organization planning
☐ Manpower requirements
analysis and planning
☐ Personnel administration
☐ Recruiting
☐ Performance specifications

Primarily about Things

- ☐ Physics
- ☐ Astronomy
- ☐ Computer programming
- ☐ Knowledge of a particular computer and its applications
- ☐ Design engineering
- ☐ Interior decorating
- ☐ How to run a particular machine
- ☐ Horticulture
- ☐ Car repairs
- ☐ Industrial applications
- ☐ Government contracts
- ☐ Maintenance
- ☐ Financial planning and management
- ☐ Bookkeeping
- ☐ Fiscal analysis, controls, reductions and programming
- ☐ Accounting
- ☐ Taxes
- ☐ R & D program and project management
- ☐ Merchandising
- ☐ Systems analysis
- ☐ Packaging
- ☐ Distribution
- ☐ Marketing/sales

Other Fields (not easily categorized)

- ☐ Principles of art
- ☐ Cinema
- ☐ Principles of recording
- ☐ Knowledge of foreign countries (which ones?)
- ☐ Musical knowledge and taste
- ☐ Graphic arts
- ☐ Photography
- ☐ Broadcasting
- ☐ How to make videos
- ☐ Linguistics or languages
- ☐ Spanish
- ☐ Music
- ☐ Policy development
- ☐ Religion

You will of course want to know if you can put down some field that you are not yet knowledgeable about: what we would call a field of *interest*, which you think you would love to learn about and use in your future ideal job. Well, sure, if you are absolutely, one hundred per cent, planning on studying that field in the near future. Or if you want to find a volunteer job or an apprenticeship where you could pick up knowledge of that field *on the job*. But let's not just talk about what you do not yet have; in addition to these **do** list fields you already know something about.

When you are all done listing or checking off all the fields you already know something about, **then** go back over the list and check your favorites, as well as cross out the ones you just hate. And, from among your favorites, pick the ten that you feel are **most** important to you to be able to use in your future ideal job, (from both the chart *and* this list), and copy these ten onto the right hand side of the petal called *Tools or Means: 2* (pages 48–49 *in their order of importance to you, if you can. Use the Prioritizing Grid if you need to (on page 14).*

When you are done, you are now ready to move on to:

Step Six: My Favorite Kinds Of Things That I Like To Work With

If you checked any skills with Things, as your favorites, in Step Three, it is important that you now specify *what kind* of Things you prefer to work with.

Following is such a list of Things. Put a check mark in front of any word that describes *things* you particularly like (or think you would particularly like) to use, or act upon, or help produce in your work. Add any others that may occur to you, which are not on the list. Then when you are done checking, pick the ten that you think are **most** important, and copy them onto the Petal on pages 58–59, in your order of preference. *"I would most enjoy working with this thing in my ideal job; next this thing; next this thing;"* etc. Use the Prioritizing Grid if you need to (on page 14).

Things I Enjoy Working With:

Types of Material
☐ Paper
☐ Pottery
☐ Pewter
☐ Paraffin
☐ Papier-mâché
☐ Wood
☐ Other crafts materials
☐ Bronze
☐ Brass
☐ Cast iron, ironworks
☐ Steel
☐ Aluminum
☐ Rubber
☐ Plywood
☐ Bricks
☐ Cement
☐ Concrete, cinder-blocks
☐ Plastics
☐ Textiles
☐ Cloth
☐ Felt
☐ Hides
☐ Synthetics
☐ Elastic
☐ Crops
☐ Plants
☐ Trees

Types of Manufactured stuff
☐ Machines
☐ Tools
☐ Toys
☐ Equipment
☐ Controls, gauges
☐ Products

☐ Housing Items
☐ Tents
☐ Trailers
☐ Apartments
☐ Houses
☐   Chimneys
☐   Columns
☐   Domes
☐   Carpenter's tools
☐   Paint
☐   Wallpaper
☐   Heating elements, furnaces
☐   Carpeting
☐   Fire extinguishers, fire
    alarms, burglar alarms
☐   Household items
☐   Furniture
☐   Beds
☐   Sheets, blankets, electric
    blankets
☐   Laundry
☐   Washing machines, dryers
☐   Washday products, bleach
☐   Kitchen appliances,
    refrigerators, microwaves,
    ovens, dishwashers,
    compactors
☐   Kitchen tools
☐   Dishes
☐   Pots and pans
☐   Can openers
☐   Bathtubs
☐   Soaps
☐   Cosmetics
☐   Toiletries
☐   Drugs
☐   Towels
☐   Tools, power tools

☐ Old Equipment
☐   Clocks
☐   Telescopes
☐   Microscopes

☐ **Foods or Food Manufacturing Equipment**
☐ Wells, cisterns
☐ Meats
☐ Breads and other baked goods
☐ Health foods
☐ Vitamins
☐ Dairy equipment
☐ Winemaking equipment

☐ **Clothing Items**
☐ Clothing
☐ Raingear, umbrellas
☐ Spinning wheels, looms
☐ Sewing machines
☐ Patterns, safety pins, buttons, zippers
☐ Dyes
☐ Shoes

☐ **Electrical and Electronics**
☐ Radios
☐ Records
☐ Phonographs
☐ Stereos
☐ Tape recorders
☐ Cameras
☐ Television cameras
☐ Television sets
☐ Videotape recorders
☐ Movie cameras, film
☐ Electronic devices
☐ Electronic games
☐ Lie detectors
☐ Radar equipment

☐ **Amusement, recreation**
☐ Games
☐ Cards
☐ Board games, checkers, chess, Monopoly, etc.
☐ Kites
☐ Gambling devices or machines

☐ **Musical Instruments**
☐ Specify:

☐ **Financial Things**
☐ Calculators
☐ Adding machines
☐ Cash registers
☐ Financial records
☐ Money

☐ **Office Related Things**
☐ PBX switchboards
☐ Desks, tables
☐ Desktop supplies
☐ Pens, ink, felt-tip, ballpoint
☐ Pencils, black, red or other
☐ Typewriter
☐ Computers
☐ Copying machines, mimeograph machines, printers

☐ **Communication Things**
☐ Telephones, answering machines
☐ Cellular phones
☐ Telegraph
☐ Fax machines, teleprinters
☐ Voice mail machines
☐ Ship-to-shore radio, shortwave, walkie-talkies

☐ **Printing Materials**
☐ Printing presses, type, ink

☐ **Art Materials**
☐ Woodcuts, engravings, lithographs
☐ Paintings, drawings, silk screens

☐ **Reading Materials**
☐ Books, braille books
☐ Newspapers
☐ Magazines

☐ **Educational Materials**
☐   Transparencies

☐ **Manufacturing or Warehouse Supplies**
☐   Dollies, handtrucks
☐   Containers
☐   Bottles
☐   Cans
☐   Boxes
☐   Automatic machines
☐   Valves, switches, buttons
☐   Cranks, wheels, gears, levers
☐   Hoists, cranes

☐ **Things that produce Light**
☐   Matches
☐   Candles
☐   Lanterns, oil lamps
☐   Light bulbs, fluorescent lights
☐   Laser beams

☐ **Energy Things**
☐   Fuel cells
☐   Batteries
☐   Transformers, electric motors, dynamos
☐   Engines, gas, diesel
☐   Windmills
☐   Waterwheels
☐   Water turbines
☐   Gas turbines
☐   Steam turbines
☐   Steam engines
☐   Dynamite
☐   Nuclear reactors

☐ **Transportation Things**
☐   Land
☐   Roads
☐   Bicycles
☐   Motorcycles
☐   Mopeds
☐   Automobiles
☐   Parking meters
☐   Traffic lights
☐   Trains
☐   Subways

☐   Air
☐   Gliders
☐   Balloons
☐   Airplanes
☐   Parachutes
☐   Sea
☐   Rivers
☐   Lakes
☐   Streams
☐   Canals
☐   Ocean
☐   Boats
☐   Steamships
☐   Other vehicles

☐ **Medical Materials or Equipment**
☐   Medicines
☐   Vaccines
☐   Anesthetics
☐   Thermometers
☐   Hearing aids
☐   Dental equipment
☐   X-ray machines
☐   False parts of the human body
☐   Spectacles, glasses, contact lenses

☐ **Gym Equipment**

☐ **Sports Equipment**
☐   Fishing rods, fishhooks, bait
☐   Traps, guns

☐ **Gardening or Farm Equipment**
☐   Garden tools
☐   Shovels
☐   Picks
☐   Rakes
☐   Lawnmowers
☐   Ploughs
☐   Threshing machines, reapers, harvesters
☐   Fertilizers
☐   Pesticides
☐   Weed killers

The Sixth Petal

Tools or Means: 3

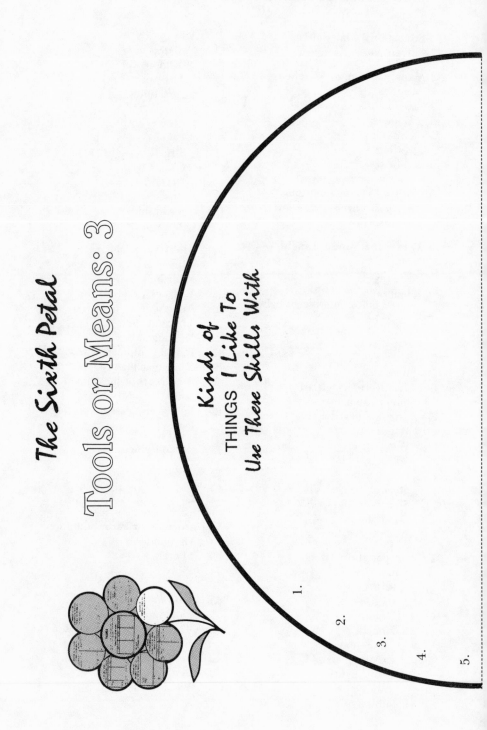

Kinds of
THINGS I Like To
Use These Skills With

1.

2.

3.

4.

5.

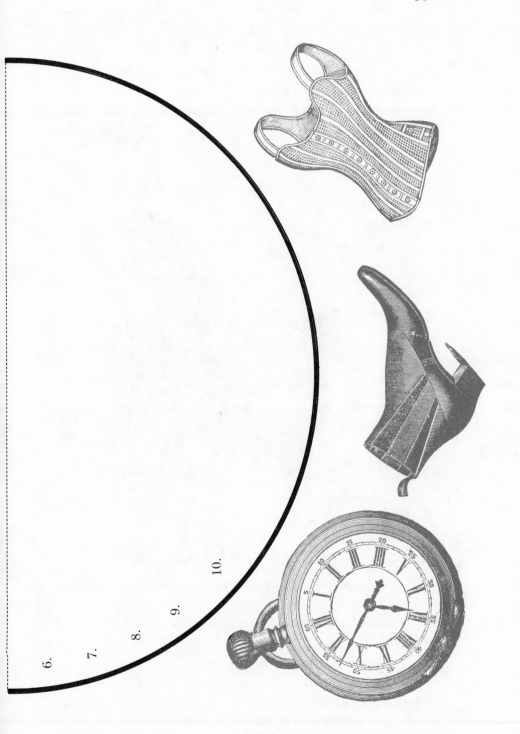

Step Seven: My Favorite Outcomes, Immediate and Long-range

Now that you know:

• what your favorite skills are, and

• what **things**, **people**, and **information** you most like to use these skills on, as well as

• what physical and spiritual **setting** you do your most effective work in,

we turn to the question of outcomes.

In the world of work, it is not enough merely to keep busy. One must be keeping busy for some purpose. We are talking about **outcomes**, or **where does it all lead to?** In the world of work, this is often called "the bottom line." I remember some years ago sending out two of my staff to find some materials for me, and after four hours' fruitless search, one turned to the other and said, "Well let's go back. At least we tried." And the other replied, "Unfortunately, in the world of work you're not usually rewarded for *trying*; you're only rewarded for *succeeding*." So they kept on, until they found what they were looking for. This underlines the point here: generally speaking, when you set about to use your skills in the world of work, you must be aiming at some **result** -- in accordance with some **purpose** or **goal**, defined by either you or the organization (preferably *both*).

So, look at the Petal on the next page. There you will see that *Outcomes* divides into two parts: **Immediate** and **Long-range**.

Immediate Results of Your Work

Immediate results, at your place of work, is a matter of: "At the work I'd most love to do, what result am I aiming at? Do I want to help produce a **product**, or do I want to help offer some **service** to people, or do I want to help gather, manage, or disseminate **information** to people? Or all three? Or two? And in what order of priority? Do I think the world basically needs me to help it have: more information, or more service, or more of some product -- such as food, clothing, or shelter?

Once you've answered that, the next question *of course* is: **what** product, or service, or information?

Well, the *what* is relatively easy to answer (I said *relatively*). If your preferred outcome is some **product** that you'd like to help produce or market, you'll probably find it identified on your *Favorite Things* petal, on pages 58–59. If your preferred outcome is some **service** to people, you'll probably find it identified on your *Favorite People* petal, on pages 44–45. And if your preferred outcome is some kind of **information** that you'd like to help gather, manage, or disseminate, you'll probably find it identified on your *Favorite Information* petal, on pages 48–49.

Another way of looking at this subject of Immediate Outcomes is to study your seven stories, to see what central motivation seems always to be driving you, what one result you seem always to be reaching for -- above all others. Here is how to discover that:

(continued on page 64.)

The Seventh Petal

Outcomes

Immediate

At the work I'd most love to do,
do I want to help produce a **product**
or do I want to help offer some **service** to people,
or do I want to help gather, manage or disseminate **information** to
people? Or two? Or all three? And what kind of product, service, or info?

And, what do I see as my central driving motivation in whatever job I take, or in whatever career I pursue?

Long-range

My long-range goals for my life -- the things I want to do, or the goals
I'd like to accomplish -- before I die, are:

Outcomes: The Central Motivation -- One Result

*Go through your seven stories and underline in purple all your verbs.
See which of the verbs below get repeated over and over again. These
describe **the one result** that you are always attempting to reach, **the
one outcome** that you find to be your chief and most coveted reward,
in all you do. You, of course, don't want to be pinned down to just
one; you want to be able to choose three, or four, or more. Fine, just
prioritize them afterward on a prioritizing grid.*

Acquire / Possess *(Money / Things / Status / People)* Wants to have own
. . . baby, toys, possessions, houses, family.

Be in Charge / Command *(of Others / Things / Organization)* Wants to
be on top, in authority, in the saddle -- where it can be determined
how things will be done . . .

Combat / Prevail *(over Adversaries / Evil / Opposing Philosophies)* Wants
to come against the bad guys, entrenched status quo, old technology . . .

Develop / Build *(Structures / Technical Things)* Wants to make something where there was nothing. . . .

Excel / Be the Best *(versus: Others / Conventional Standards)* Wants to
be the fastest, first, longest, earliest, or more complicated, better
than others . . .

Exploit / Achieve Potential *(of Situations / Markets / Things / People)*
Sees a silk purse, a giant talent, a hot product, or a promising market before the fact . . .

Gain Response / Influence Behavior *(from People / Through People)*
Wants dogs, cats, people, and groups to react to their touch . . .

Gain Recognition / Attention *(from Peers / Public Authority)* Wants to
wave at the cheering crowd, appear in the newspaper, be known,
dance in the spotlight . . .

Improve / Make Better *(Oneself / Others / Work / Organizations)* Makes
what is marginal, good; what is good, better; what makes a little
money, make a lot of money. . . .

Make the Team / Grade *(Established by Others or the System)* Gains ac-
cess to the varsity, Eagle Scout rank, Silver Circle, Thirty-ninth Ma-
sonic Order, the country club, executive dining room . . .

Meet Needs / Fulfill Expectations *(that are Demanded / Needed / or
Inherent)* Strives to meet specifications, shipping schedules, what the
customer wants, what the boss has expressed . . .

Make Work / Make Effective *(Things / Systems / Operations)* Fixes what
is broken, changes what is out-of-date, redesigns what has been
poorly conceived. . . .

Master / Perfect *(Some Subject / Skill / Equipment / Objects)* Goes after
rough edges, complete domination of a technique, total control over
the variables . . .

Organize / Operate *(Business / Team / Product Line)* The entrepre-
neur, the beginner of new businesses . . .

Overcome / Persevere *(Obstacles / Handicaps / Unknown Odds)* Goes after hungry tigers with a popgun, concave mountains with slippery boots. . . .

Pioneer / Explore *(Technology / Cultures / Ideas)* Presses through established lines, knowledge, boundaries . . .

Serve / Help *(People / Organizations / Causes)* Carries the soup, ministers to the wounded, helps those in need . . .

Shape / Influence *(Material / Policy / People)* Wants to leave a mark, to cause change, to impact . . .

(Adapted by Richard N. Bolles from Miller, Arthur F., and Mattson, Ralph T., The Truth About You: Discover what you should be doing with your life, 1st ed., 1977, pp. 68–69. Not to be reproduced without written permission from Arthur Miller, People Management Inc., 10 Station Street, Simsbury, Conn. 06070.)

The Long-range Results of Your Work

As a result of **all** the work you do here on earth, what results or outcome do you want to achieve by the time that you die? What goals do you want to accomplish, what things do you want to do? Your answer to this should be written out, thoughtfully, on a single piece of scratch paper (no more than one page, please) -- and then the most important points in your statement should be copied onto the bottom part of the petal on pages 62–63. Go back, also, and look at your philosophy of life, on page 16.

Incidentally, if while you are writing this statement, you find yourself setting down some long-range goals that really have nothing to do with *your work* as such, but have to do more with your overall *life* -- such as, "Before I die, I want to travel all over the world" -- write them down *anyway*. You just never know when a job might be offered to you somewhere down the road that would make it possible for you to achieve some of your **life**-goals, and not just your work or achievement-goals.

And now on to the last step in your putting together a picture of your ideal job:

Step Eight: My Favorite Rewards at Work

If you look at page 68-69, you will see the final petal of your *flower* picture of the ideal job for you. It is entitled "Rewards." Virtually all of us hope for some reward from our job that is different than, and distinguishable from, *the outcomes* which we saw in the previous Step. That is to say, in addition to producing a product, service, or information, we (usually) want our work to put bread on our table, clothes on our back, and a roof over our head -- at a minimum.

The petal speaks of **Level** and **Salary**. It asks you to think out what is the *minimum* salary you would need from your next job or career, and what is the *maximum* salary you would like to have if things were ideal.

Hand in hand with *salary* goes the question of *level*. If you aspire, in matters of salary, to $70,000 a year, but you aspire, in the matter of level, to being an office boy, there is something flawed about your dream. Level and salary usually go hand in hand. Office boys don't make $70,000 a year.

On this petal, salary is relatively easy to figure out. Minimum is what you simply *must* make, or you will starve. It requires a little budget figuring, and that's all. Maximum is what you would *like* to make. It requires a little searching of your daydreams, and that's all.

Level is harder to figure out. To some degree, it's what you find out as you conduct your informational interviewing after you have completed this booklet. For example, let us say that you discover from your flower picture, that your ideal job would involve doing research into how one prolongs human life. As you visit the various places that are involved in such research, you discover that an apprentice researcher makes barely your minimum desired salary. A team member with ten years' experience makes $10,000 more than your minimum salary, while only a senior researcher who is head of a research team makes the maximum salary that you have put on your petal here. It is at this point (and this point only) that you can really fill out the level part of this petal: e.g., apprentice researcher.

But, there are some questions about *level* -- let's call them "some preliminary hunches" that you *can* put down, even now. For example, in your ideal job do you want to work:

☐ by yourself and for yourself;

☐ by yourself but for another person or organization;

☐ in *tandem* with one other person;

☐ as a member of a team of equals;

☐ as a member of a hierarchy where you carry out directions;

☐ as a member of a hierarchy where you are the boss or supervisor or owner;

☐ or what?

Jot down, on the petal, as many ideas or hunches as occur to you at the moment. You can always change them later (as indeed, you can change *any* petal) after you have conducted your own research or informational interviewing about your *flower* picture.

At the bottom of this petal, you will see that space has been provided for you to add any other rewards that you would like your ideal job to give you. What do we mean by this? Well, many people hope their job will give them more by way of reward, than just money. *For example* (put a check mark in front of any that apply to you):

☐ Social contact	☐ Respect
☐ A chance to help others	☐ Adventure
☐ A chance to bring others closer to God	☐ Challenge
☐ Intellectual stimulation	☐ Influence
☐ A chance to use my expertise	☐ Security
☐ A chance to make decisions	☐ Independence
☐ A chance to be creative	☐ Wealth
☐ A chance to exercise leadership	☐ Power
☐ A chance to be popular	☐ Fame

Jot down any others that may occur to you, which are not on this list. When you are done, rank them in their order of importance to you (you may use the Prioritizing Grid, on page 14, if you wish), and then copy them in order, on the bottom part of this petal.

The Eighth Petal

Rewards

Salary and Level
I Want/Need

LEVEL		SALARY
MAX		

Other rewards I would like this job to give me:

MIN

Conclusion: Putting It All Together

Now that you have completed all of the petals, it is time to put them all together on one piece of paper. Why do you need to put all the petals together? Because, your ideal job is not going to be found lying about the countryside in eight separate pieces; it will be a unity, and so must your picture of it be, that you carry in your mind (or in your notebook) as you go job-hunting.

So, don't leave the filled-out picture of the petals as they presently are -- all separated from each other, lying on separate sheets in this booklet. Please cut out the circles of each petal and paste them, or photocopy them -- all of them -- onto one piece of paper.

Obviously, you will need a large sheet of blank paper on which to do this. You may make this sheet most easily by simply taping together nine sheets of plain 8½ × 11 inch paper as shown here:

Or, if you want to avoid all this taping, you may go to any art supply or large stationery store, and buy a sheet of paper or cardboard there that is about 24 × 36 inches in size. When you have this larger paper, **please** paste (or copy) all your filled-out petals onto it, so that the overall picture resembles the Flower Picture on the next page:

This is what your Flower should look like, when you have it all pasted together: For a successful career-change, or a successful job-hunt, you ***must*** know the answers to these questions. You must, you must, you must *thus* cut down the territory that you now need to go exploring.

**You are now ready
to tackle the practical steps outlined in
Chapter 5 of *The 1990 What Color
Is Your Parachute?***

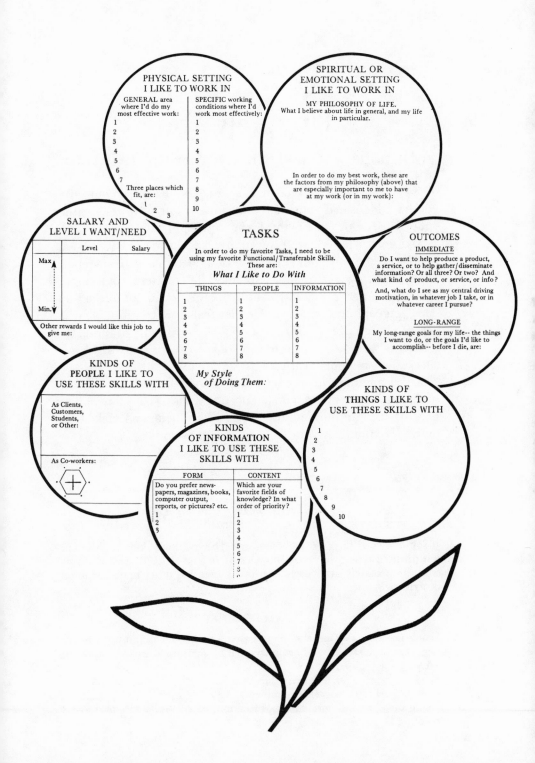

PHYSICAL SETTING I LIKE TO WORK IN

GENERAL area where I'd do my most effective work:
1
2
3
4
5
6
7

Three places which fit, are:
1
2
3

SPECIFIC working conditions where I'd work most effectively:
1
2
3
4
5
6
7
8
9
10

SPIRITUAL OR EMOTIONAL SETTING I LIKE TO WORK IN

MY PHILOSOPHY OF LIFE. What I believe about life in general, and my life in particular.

In order to do my best work, these are the factors from my philosophy (above) that are especially important to me to have at my work (or in my work):

SALARY AND LEVEL I WANT/NEED

	Level	Salary
Max		
Min.		

Other rewards I would like this job to give me:

TASKS

In order to do my favorite Tasks, I need to be using my favorite Functional/Transferable Skills. These are:
What I Like to Do With

THINGS	PEOPLE	INFORMATION
1	1	1
2	2	2
3	3	3
4	4	4
5	5	5
6	6	6
7	7	7
8	8	8

My Style of Doing Them:

OUTCOMES

IMMEDIATE

Do I want to help produce a product, a service, or to help gather/disseminate information? Or all three? Or two? And what kind of product, or service, or info?

And, what do I see as my central driving motivation, in whatever job I take, or in whatever career I pursue?

LONG-RANGE

My long-range goals for my life-- the things I want to do, or the goals I'd like to accomplish-- before I die, are:

KINDS OF PEOPLE I LIKE TO USE THESE SKILLS WITH

As Clients, Customers, Students, or Other:

As Co-workers:

KINDS OF INFORMATION I LIKE TO USE THESE SKILLS WITH

FORM	CONTENT
Do you prefer newspapers, magazines, books, computer output, reports, or pictures? etc.	Which are your favorite fields of knowledge? In what order of priority?
1	1
2	2
3	3
	4
	5
	6
	7
	8
	9

KINDS OF THINGS I LIKE TO USE THESE SKILLS WITH

1
2
3
4
5
6
7
8
9
10

Uniquely You

A Dictionary of Skill Synonyms or Related Words

This is a supplemental section. It is designed to be used only **after** you have identified your skills **and** chosen your favorites -- either your Top Ten or your Eight, Eight, and Eight.

You don't need to use this section at all, if you are basically satisfied with the way your skills were described on the Transferable Skills charts (pages 28–33). But most job-hunters, and career-changers in particular, **will** want to get their skills out of the standard language and into language they feel more comfortable with, because it describes their uniqueness. If you are one of those, this section is for you. You need only look up those skills which you checked off as your favorites.

See if anything in this section describes the skill you actually have, in a better way. You do not need to slavishly copy any phrases here. If you can think of any way to adapt them, and make them even more uniquely your own, by all means do so.

Skills with Things

If some of your favorite skills were with **Things**, those skills are listed below (in **bold** type), with the synonyms or related skills (if any) in regular type, immediately after each. Circle any that you think more accurately describe what it is you do.

I AM GOOD AT

Using my hands or fingers: good with my hands; feeling, fingering, having manual dexterity, gathering, receiving, separating, sorting, applying, pressing
Having great finger dexterity: having keen sense of touch, keyboarding, typing, playing (a musical instrument)
Using my eyes and hands in coordination: balancing, juggling, drawing, painting

Motor/physical coordination with my whole body: possessing fine motor coordination, raising, lifting, carrying, pushing, pulling, moving, unloading, walking, running, backpacking, swimming, hiking, mountaineering, skiing
Having agility, speed, strength or stamina: displaying great physical agility, possessing great strength, demonstrating outstanding endurance, maintaining uncommon physical fitness, acting as bodyguard
Crafting, sewing, weaving, hammering, etc.: knitting, collecting
Cutting, carving or chiseling: logging, mining, drawing samples from the earth
Fashioning, molding, shaping or sculpting: working (materials)
Finishing, painting, refinishing, or restoring: binding, sandblasting, grinding
Precision working with my hands: making miniatures, skilled at working in the micro-universe
Washing, cleaning or preparing:
Handling, or expediting: using particular tools (say which), placing, guiding, receiving, shipping, distributing, delivering
Making, producing, manufacturing (cooking): having great culinary skills
Maintaining, preserving, or repairing, objects, tools, instruments:
Precision working with tools or instruments: precise attainment of set limits, tolerances, or standards; having great dexterity with small instruments (e.g., tweezers); keypunching; drilling; enjoy working within precise limits or standards of accuracy
Setting up or assembling: clearing, laying, installing, displaying
Operating, controlling, or driving: piloting, navigating, guiding, steering, mastering machinery against its will
Tending, minding, feeding, or emptying: monitoring machines or valves, giving continuous attention to, regulating controls of, watching to make sure nothing goes wrong, making a ready response in any emergency, checking, pushing buttons, starting, flipping switches, switching, adjusting controls, turning knobs, making adjustments when machine threatens to malfunction, placing, inserting, stacking, loading, dumping, removing, disposing of
Maintaining, cleaning or repairing equipment, machinery, or vehicles: changing, refilling, tuning, adjusting, fitting, doing preventative maintenance, trouble-shooting, restoring, fixing
Breaking down, disassembling, or salvaging: mopping up, cleaning up, knocking down
Constructing or reconstructing: erecting, putting together
Modeling or remodeling: able to perform magic on a room
Having a green thumb, causing growing things to flourish: helping to grow, farming, digging, plowing, tilling, seeding, planting, nurturing, groundskeeping, landscaping, weeding, harvesting
Having skills with animals, raising, training, or treating, etc: animal training, ranching, sensing, persuading, etc. *With higher animals, the skills used are very similar to people skills (see below).*

Skills with People

If some of your favorite skills were with **People**, those skills are listed below (in **bold** type), with the synonyms or related skills (if any) in regular type, immediately after each. Circle any that you think more accurately describe what it is you do.

WITH INDIVIDUALS,
I AM GOOD AT

Taking instructions, serving, or helping: following detailed instructions, rendering support services, preparing (something for someone), hostessing, waiting on tables, protecting, rendering services to, dealing patiently with difficult people

Communicating well in conversation, in person or on the phone: hearing and answering questions perceptively, adept at two-way dialogue, being sensitive and responsive to the feelings of others, empathizing, showing warmth, good telephoning skills, developing warmth over the telephone, creating an atmosphere of acceptance, keen ability to put self in someone else's shoes, signaling, talking, telling, informing, giving instructions, exchanging information

Communicating well in writing: (see above), also: expressing with clarity, verbalizing cogently, uncommonly warm letter composition

Instructing, teaching, tutoring, or training individuals: guiding, interpreting and expressing facts and ideas

Advising, coaching, counseling, mentoring, empowering: facilitating personal growth and development; helping people identify their problems, needs, and solutions; interpreting others' dreams; raising people's self-esteem

Diagnosing, treating, or healing: prescribing, attending, caring for, nursing, ministering to, caring for the handicapped, having true therapeutic abilities, having healing abilities, powerful in prayer, rehabilitating, curing, raising people's self-esteem

Referring people, or helping two people to link up: recommending, making and using contacts effectively, acting as a resource broker, finding people or other resources, adept at calling in other experts or helpers as needed

Assessing, evaluating, screening, or selecting individuals: having accurate gut reactions, sizing up other people perceptively, quickly assessing what's going on, realistically assessing people's needs, perceptive in identifying and assessing the potential of others, monitoring behavior through watching, critical evaluation, and feedback

Persuading, motivating, recruiting, or selling individuals: influencing, moving, inspiring, displaying charisma, inspiring trust, evoking loyalty, convincing, motivating, developing rapport or trust, recruiting talent or leadership, attracting skilled, competent and creative people, enlisting, demonstrating (a product), selling tangibles or intangibles

Representing others, interpreting others' ideas or language: translating jargon into relevant and meaningful terms, helping others to express their views, speaking a foreign language fluently, serving as an interpreter, clarifying values and goals of others, expert at liaison roles, representing a majority or minority group in a larger meeting or assembly

WITH GROUPS,
I AM GOOD AT

Communicating effectively
to a group or a multitude, by . . .

Using words expressively in speaking or writing: outstanding writing skills; making oral presentations; exceptional speaking ability; addressing large or small groups confidently; very responsive to audience's moods or ideas; thinking quickly on my feet; speechwriting, playwriting and writing with humor, fun and flair; employing humor in describing my experiences; ability to vividly describe people or scenes so that others can visualize them; very explicit and concise writing; making people think; doing excellent promotional writing; creating imaginative advertising and publicity programs; keeping superior minutes of meetings

Making presentations in person, or on TV or film: using voice tone and rhythm as unusually effective tools of communication, giving radio or TV presentations, giving briefings, making reports

Performing, entertaining, amusing, or inspiring: exhibiting showmanship, having strong theatrical sense, understudying, provoking laughter, making people laugh, distracting, diverting

Signing, miming, acting, singing, or playing an instrument: dramatizing, modeling, dancing, playing music, giving poetry readings, relating seemingly disparate ideas by means of words or actions, exceptionally good at facial expressions or body language to express thoughts or feelings eloquently

Playing games, or a particular game, leading others in recreation or exercise: excellent at sports; excellent at a particular sport (tennis, gymnastics, running, swimming, golf, baseball, football); helping others to get fit; creating, planning, and organizing outdoor activities; leading backpacking, hiking, camping, mountain-climbing expeditions; outdoor survival skills; excellent at traveling

Teaching, training, or designing educational events: lecturing; explaining; instructing; enlightening; demonstrating; showing; detailing; modeling (desired behavior); patient teaching; organizing and administering in-house training events; planning and carrying out well-run seminars, workshops, or meetings; fostering a stimulating learning environment; ability to shape the atmosphere of a place so that it is warm, pleasant, and comfortable; instilling in people a love of the subject being taught; explaining difficult or complex concepts or ideas; putting things in perspective; showing others how to take advantage of a resource; helping others to experience something; making distinctive visual presentations

Guiding a group discussion, conveying warmth: skilled at chairing meetings; group-facilitating; refusing to put people into slots or categories; treating others as equals, without regard to education, authority, or position; discussing; conferring; exchanging information; drawing out people; encouraging people; helping people make their own discoveries; helping people identify their own intelligent self-interest; adept at two-way dialogue; ability to hear and answer questions perceptively

Persuading a group, debating, motivating, or selling: publicizing, promoting, reasoning persuasively, influencing the ideas and attitudes of others, selling a program or course of action to decision-makers, obtaining agreement after the fact, fund-raising, arranging financing, writing a proposal, promoting or bringing about major policy changes, devising a systematic approach to goal setting

Consulting, giving advice to groups in my area of expertise: advising, giving expert advice or recommendations, trouble-shooting, giving professional advice, giving insight concerning

Managing, supervising, or running a business, fund drive, etc.: coordinating, overseeing, heading up, administering, directing, controlling (a project), conducting (an orchestra), directing (a production, or play), planning, organizing, and staging of theatrical productions, adept at planning and staging ceremonies, deft at directing creative talent, interpreting goals, promoting harmonious relations and efficiency, encouraging people, organizing my time expertly, setting up and maintaining on-time work schedules, establishing effective priorities among competing requirements, coordinating operations and details, sizing up situations, anticipating people's needs, deals well with the unexpected or critical event, skilled at allocating scarce financial resources, bringing projects in on time and within budget, able to make hard decisions

Following through, getting things done, producing: executing, carrying out decisions reached, implementing decisions, expediting, building customer loyalty, unusual ability to work self-directedly without supervision, able to handle a variety of tasks and responsibilities simultaneously and efficiently, instinctively gathering resources even before the need for them becomes clear, recognizing obsolescence of ideas or procedures before compelling evidence is yet at hand, anticipating problems or needs before they become problems, decisive in emergencies, continually searching for more responsibility, developing or building markets for ideas or products, completing, attaining objectives, meeting goals, producing results, delivering as promised, increasing productivity, making good use of feedback

Leading, taking the lead, being a pioneer: determining goals, objectives, and procedures, making policy, willing to experiment with new approaches, recognizing and utilizing the skills of others, organizing diverse people into a functioning group, unifying, energizing, team-building, delegating authority, sharing responsibility, taking manageable risks, instinctively understand political realities, acting on new information immediately, seek and seize opportunities

Initiating, starting up, founding, or establishing: originating, instituting, establishing, charting, financing startups

Negotiating between two parties, or resolving conflicts: mediating, arbitrating, bargaining, umpiring, adjudicating, renegotiating, reconciling, resolving, achieving compromise, charting mergers, getting diverse groups to work together, adept at conflict management, accepting of differing opinions, handling prima donnas tactfully and well, collaborating with colleagues skillfully, handling super-difficult individuals in situations, without stress, skilled at arriving at jointly agreed-upon decisions or policy or program or solutions, working well in a hostile environment, confronting others with touchy or difficult personal matters, treating people fairly.

Skills with Information

If some of your favorite skills were with **Information**, those skills are listed below (in **bold** type), with the synonyms or related skills (if any) in regular type, immediately after each. Circle any that you think more accurately describe what it is you do.

I AM GOOD AT

Compiling, searching, or researching: have exceptional intelligence tempered by common sense; like dealing with ideas, information and concepts; exhibit a perpetual curiosity and delight in new knowledge; relentlessly curious; have a love of printed things; reading avidly; reading ceaselessly; committed to continual personal growth, and learning; continually seeking to expose self to new experiences; love to stay current, particularly on the subjects of . . . ; continually gathering information with respect to a particular problem or area of expertise (say *what*); finding and getting things not easy to find; searching databases; discovering; discovering resources, ways, and means; investigating; detecting; surveying; identifying; ascertaining; determining; finding; assembling; compiling; gathering; collecting; surveying organizational needs; doing economic research

Gathering information by interviewing, or observing people: skilled at striking up conversations with strangers, talking easily with all kinds of people, adept at gathering information from people by talking to them, listening intently and accurately, intuiting, inquiring, questioning people gently, highly observant of people, learn from the example of others, study other people's behavior perceptively, accurately assessing public moods

Gathering information by studying, or observing things: paying careful attention to, being very observant, keenly aware of surroundings, examining, concentrating, focusing on minutiae

Having an acute sense of hearing, smell, taste, or sight: ability to distinguish different musical notes, perfect pitch, having uncommonly fine sense of rhythm, possessing color discrimination of a very high order, possessing instinctively excellent taste in design, arrangement, and color

Imagining, inventing, creating, or designing new ideas: devising, generating, innovating, formulating, conceptualizing, having conceptual ability of a high order, hypothesizing, discovering, conceiving new concepts, approaches, interpretations, being an idea man or woman, having "ideaphoria," demonstrating originality, continually conceiving, generating and developing innovative and creative ideas, creative imagining, possessed of great imagination, having imagination and the courage to use it, improvising on the spur of the moment, composing (music), continually conceiving, generating and developing music, continually creating new ideas for systems, methods, and procedures

Copying, and/or comparing similarities or differences: addressing, posting, making comparisons, checking, proofreading, perceiving identities or divergencies, developing a standard or model, estimating (e.g., the speed of a moving object), comparing with previous data

Computing, working with numbers, doing accounting: counting, taking inventory, counting with high accuracy, having arithmetical skills, calculating, performing rapid and accurate manipulation of numbers, in my head or on paper, having very sophisticated mathematical abilities, solving statistical problems, using numbers as a reasoning tool, preparing financial reports, estimating, budgeting, projecting, ordering, purchasing, acquiring, auditing, maintaining fiscal controls

Analyzing, breaking down into its parts: reasoning, dissecting, atomizing, figuring out, finding the basic units, breaking into its basic elements, defining cause-and-effect relationships, doing financial or fiscal analysis, doing effective cost analysis

Organizing, classifying, systematizing, and/or prioritizing: putting things in order, bringing order out of chaos (with ideas, data, or things), putting into working order, perceiving common denominators, giving a definite structure and working order to things, forming into a whole with connected and interdependent parts, formulating, defining, clustering, collating, tabulating, protecting, keeping confidential

Planning, laying out a step-by-step process for achieving a goal: determining the sequence of tasks after reviewing pertinent data or requirements, planning on the basis of learnings from the past, determining the sequence of operations, establishing logical, sequential methods to accomplish stated goals, making arrangements for the functioning of a system, planning for change

Adapting, translating, computer programming, developing, or improving: updating, expanding, improving, upgrading, applying, arranging (e.g., music), redesigning, improvising, adjusting, interpreting, extrapolating, projecting, forecasting, creating a new form of something, taking what others have developed and applying it to new situations, making practical applications of theoretical ideas, deriving applications from other people's ideas, able to see the commercial possibilities in a concept, idea, or product, revising goals, policies, and procedures, translating numbers and words into electronically coded computer data

Visualizing, drawing, painting, dramatizing, creating videos, or software: continually conceiving, generating, and developing pictures, able to visualize shapes, able to visualize in three dimensions, conceiving shapes, colors, or sounds, having form perception, skilled at symbol formation, creating symbols, conceiving symbolic or metaphoric pictures of Reality, designing, designing in wood or other media, fashioning, shaping, making models, designing handicrafts, creating poetic images, thinking in pictures, visualizing concepts, illustrating, sketching, coloring, drafting, graphing, mapping, photographing, doing computer graphics, doing mechanical drawing, able to read blueprints, able to read graphs quickly, using video or other recording equipment to produce imaginative audio/visual presentations, good at set designing

Synthesizing, combining parts into a whole: transforming apparently unrelated things or ideas, by forming them into a new whole, relating, combining, integrating, unifying, producing a clear, coherent unity, seeing 'the big picture,' always seeing things in a larger context

Problem solving, or seeing patterns among a mass of data: diagnosing, intuiting, figuring out, perceiving patterns or structures, recognizing when more information is needed before a decision can be reached, proving, disproving, validating

Deciding, evaluating, appraising, or making recommendations: love making decisions that require personal judgment, making judgments about people or data or things, keeping confidences, keeping secrets, encrypting, inspecting, studying data to determine compliance with an established norm, checking, testing, weighing, appraising, assessing, determining the fair market value of an object, reviewing, critiquing, discriminating between what is important and what is unimportant, separating the wheat from the chaff, summarizing, editing, reducing the size of a database, judging, selecting, screening, screening out, extracting, reviewing large amounts of material and extracting its essence, writing a precis, conserving, making fiscal reductions, eliminating, simplifying, consolidating

Keeping records, including recording, filming, or entering on a computer: transcribing, reproducing, imitating, keeping accurate financial records, operating a computer competently, word processing, maintaining databases

Storing, or filing, in file cabinets, microfiche, video, audio, or computer: good clerical ability

Retrieving information, ideas, data: extracting, reviewing, restoring, reporting, giving out information patiently and accurately, good at getting materials that are needed

Enabling other people to find or retrieve information: filing in a way to facilitate retrieval, classifying expertly, organizing information according to a prescribed plan, am an excellent 'resource broker'

Having a superior memory, keeping track of details: easily remember facts and figures, having a keen and accurate memory for detail, recalling people and their preferences accurately, retentive memory for rules and procedures, expert at remembering numbers and statistics accurately and for a long period, having exceedingly accurate melody recognition, exhibiting keen tonal memory, accurately reproducing sounds or tones (e.g., a foreign language, spoken without accent), easily remembering faces, accurate spatial memory, having a memory for design, having a photographic memory.

Now, you will want to finish the statement of skills in your own language, by describing **degree**. Here are some possible modifiers you may want to put in front of **the skills you are best at** *(one usually omits the words "I . . ." or "I have . . ." or "I am . . . ," which are understood)*.

- Good at . . . ,
- Exceptionally good at . . . ,
- Adept at . . . ,
- Expert at . . . ,
- Deft at . . . ,
- Excel at . . . ,
- Unusually skillful at . . . ,
- Unusual ability to . . . ,
- Skilled at . . . ,
- Demonstrated exceptional ability to . . .

When you are done with this section, before you copy them onto the *Tasks / Transferable Skills* petal on page 36f, flesh out your favorite skills, viz., adding to the verb an object and a modifier as described on page 34. In this fleshing out, the phrases above can be used as modifiers of particular skills, if they are used in their adjective or adverb form, e.g., *"Exceptional," "uncommon," "adeptly," "expertly," "skillfully," "unusually,"* and so forth.